Albatros D.Va Mercedes 170-185 h.p., span 9m, length 7.30m, two Spandau machine guns, speed 185 kph, ceiling 6,250m, endurance 2 hours. German.

Fokker D.VII Mercedes 160-180 or BMW 185 h.p., span 9m, length 7m, two Spandau machine guns, speed 188 kph, ceiling 7,000m, endurance 1½ hours. German.

Sopwith Camel Clerget 130 or Bentley 150 h.p., span 8.50m, length 5.70m, two Vickers machine guns, speed 196 kph, ceiling 7,300m, endurance 2½ hours. British.

Fokker Dr. 1 Le Rhône or Oberusel 110 h.p., span 6m, length 5.70m, two Spandau machine guns, speed 164 kph, ceiling 6,000m, endurance 1½ hours. German.

© Flammarion 1978

First English edition 1979
Macdonald Educational Ltd,
Holywell House,
Worship Street,
London EC2A 2EN

ISBN 0 356 06300 3

Printed in Italy by
A. Mondadori, Verona

Contents

Pilots

of World War 1

by MELVILLE WALLACE
illustrated by MICHAEL TURNER

Macdonald Educational

Machines to frighten horses

The British cavalry general who called airplanes "machines to frighten horses" may just have been deafened by the noise made by the ungainly pre-war aircraft, but he may also have realized that the days of the intrepid cavalry charge with lowered lances were coming to an end. Yet in at least one instance charging horsemen, like medieval knights, bloodily confronted the hated machines of the future.

Within five weeks of the outbreak of war, the German armies had swept both south and east toward the Marne, trapping a large contingent of French troops who tried to escape in the direction of the Aisne and Verdun. The German advance was accompanied by a squadron of Aviatik observation planes. Lieutenant Gironde of the 16th Dragoons learned from a peasant that there was a German air unit based at Vivières, just north of Villers Cotterêts, and decided to attack it.

In the dead of night, he dismounted half his troop only a few hundred metres from the Germans and sent them ahead to clear the way. They crawled into range, struck down a sentry and set fire to a truck, lighting the way for the charge. Sabre raised and leading his platoon of lancers at full gallop toward the planes, Gironde was met by a deadly hail of bullets from a machine gun mounted on the German staff car. Within seconds the field was strewn with the writhing bodies of dead or wounded horses and dragoons. Nevertheless, the attack had achieved its goal of destroying the enemy planes, and had given Gironde the distinction of leading one of the last cavalry charges in history.

The weapon which made air combat possible spelled doom to the cavalry, whose twin missions of observation and pursuit were soon in the hands of the airmen. By this time former cavalrymen, such as von Richthofen, Nungesser and Baracca, had become pilots and aces—the new "Knights of the Air"!

gave it a
... as the "Fokker Scourge", but by
... had been outclassed by such British pushers
... DH.2 and FE.2 and, above all, by the nippy
...ench Nieuport series. The "Bébé" Nieuport 11 and
its successor the N.17 were sesquiplanes: their upper full-span, twin spar wings were connected to a narrow lower pair by a V-shaped strut. This arrangement was designed to combine the rigidity and high lift of a ...russed biplane design with the good visibility and low ...rag of the monoplane.

The Nieuport was originally armed with only a ...gle Lewis gun over the top wing, but a synchronized ...kers was added later. With it, the Allies were able to ...in mastery of the air in 1916, and it was the plane ...hich aces such as Bishop, Ball, Baracca, Nungesser ...Guynemer won their spurs.

... advantages of the sesquiplane were quickly seen ...rman designers: Albatros modified their plywood-...ed D.I and D.II accordingly to produce the ...nd D.V models, used by the "Circuses" until ... by the even more gaudily painted Fokker ...s and the rugged D.VII.

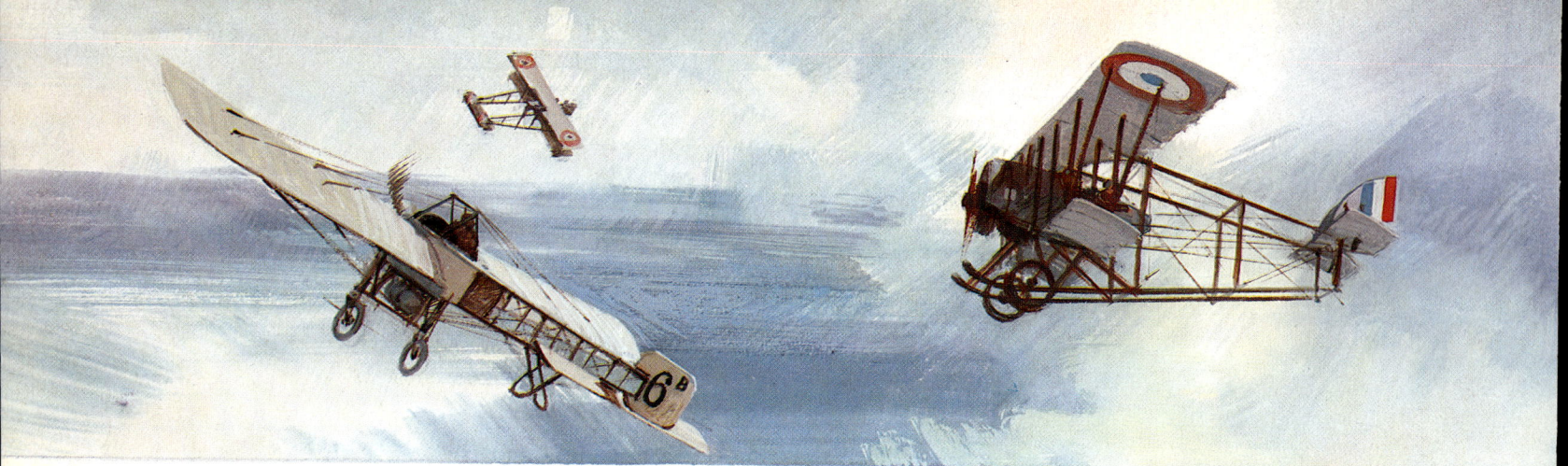

A new weapon takes off

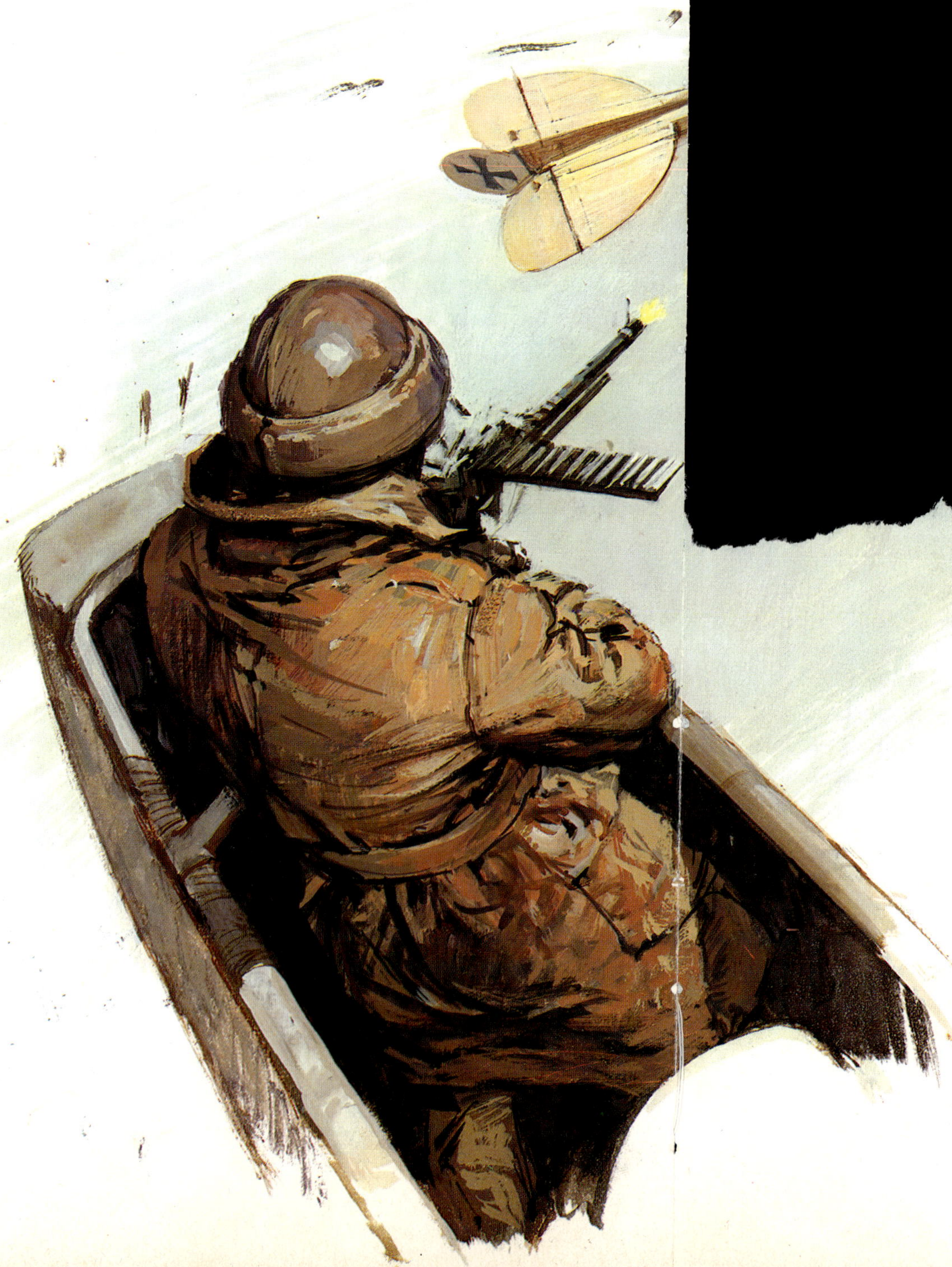

Despite General Foch's pre-war statement that airplanes were mere playthings, they soon proved their usefulness as the army's "eyes". It was British pilots who spotted the gap in the German lines near Mons which enabled their troops to close ranks with the French.

During the first four days of September, flights of French reconnaissance planes scoured the countryside to the north and west of Paris, rushing back to General Gallieni's headquarters to report the enemy's position. One pilot after another reported no troops west of the Oise river and that the entire right wing of the German army seemed to be swerving eastward. Relying on this information, Gallieni sent his taxi-riding garrison in that direction. On the evening of the 4th General Joffre informed his staff: "Gentlemen, we will fight on the Marne." Within ten days the Kaiser's push had come to a halt; Paris (and France) were saved. Thus the first victory on the Marne owed much to the pilots and observers in their Blériots, Voisins, Caudrons and Farmans.

Considering the limited range of the light and fragile aircraft available, it no wonder that the Allied General Staff saw them as passive observers, their fears focused on Imperial Germany's impressive fleet of Zeppelins. Then, within ten days of the outbreak of war, the French successfully bombed the Zeppelin shed at Metz. Shortly afterwards British Lieutenant Marix, flying a Sopwith Tabloid, bombed and completely destroyed the newly commissioned Z.XIX.

Lieutenant Rumney Samson of the Royal Navy achieved a still more impressive feat when he personally

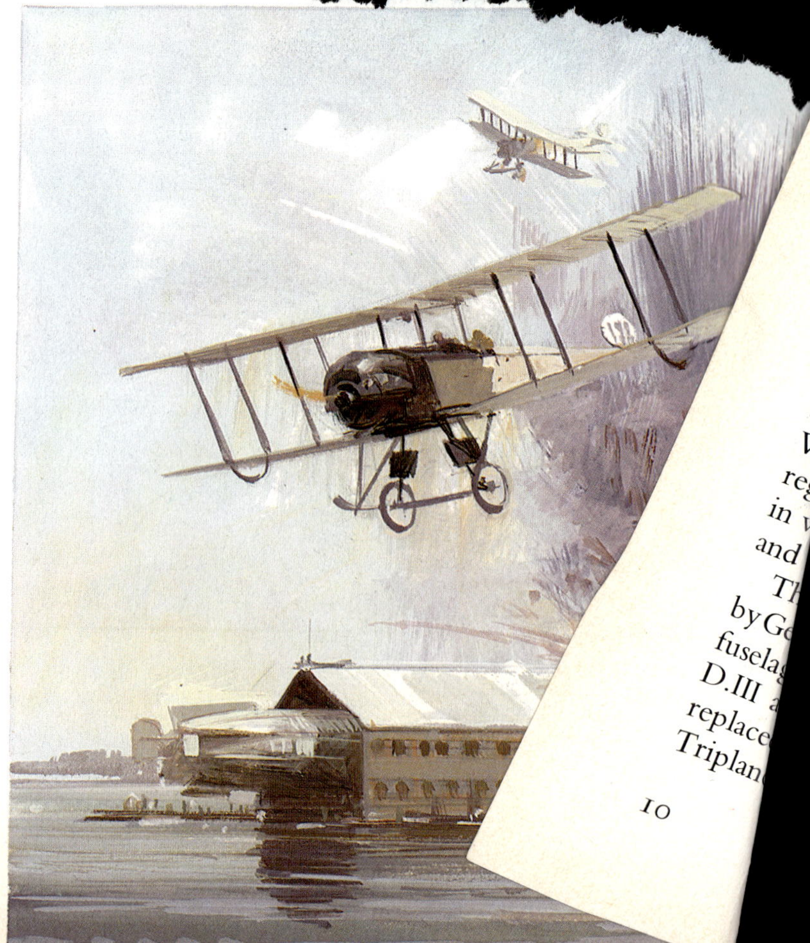

si
Vi
reg
in v
and
Th
by G
fuselag
D.III a
replace
Triplan

reconnoitred the Zeppelin factory at Friedrichshafen, rowing across Lake Constance after making his way through Switzerland incognito. Returning to his base in Belfort, he and his men took off in three Avro 504s and successfully followed a carefully mapped-out course avoiding neutral territory via Mulhouse and across the Black Forest to Schaffhausen before turning south toward Lake Constance.

It soon became clear that denying the skies to enemy planes was vitally important and that this could not be done with unarmed aircraft. At first pilots used their sidearms and rifles to fire at each other, but when Gabriel Voisin mounted an infantry machine gun on one of his pushers the fighter was born.

On 5th October 1914, not far from Reims, Franz and Quénault spotted an Aviatik two-seater headed for home. Quénault fired two clips from the tripod over his pilot's head before his Hotchkiss jammed. The German plane spiralled to the ground, the first victim in the history of aerial combat. As well as medals, Franz and Quénault were rewarded with their victim's engine, the sale of which provided delicacies for their mess for the next two months!

Below: Dipping to within three metres of the water to avoid detection, they then soared to 400 metres before diving on the well-defended Zeppelin factory and gasworks. The result was a tremendous explosion and flames leaping high into the air.

Aircraft design and development

Fokker
"Eindecker"

Speed, manoeuvrability and firepower were the three essential characteristics of a fighter and so were avidly sought by the warring powers. Captured enemy planes in good condition were immediately tested by ace pilots. Any good points were then noted and incorporated into a new generation of combat aircraft. Even Fokker's famous "Eindecker" was based on a captured French Morane monoplane which the Dutch designer dismantled and copied. Better flight characteristics were achieved mainly through adding ribs to the wing structure, thus improving airflow: however, no change was made to the old system of wing-warping. The resulting tangle of drag-producing wires combined with its low-powered engine to make the plane slow and completely unmanoeuvrable at high altitudes.

The E.1's forward firing machine gun formidable reputation
early 1916 it
as the
Fr

Below: Extremely compact, with pilot, engine, fuel, guns and wings all concentrated well forward, the Sopwith Camel's legendary manoeuvrability was further enhanced by huge ailerons on all four wingtips and the torque effect produced by its whirling rotary engine.

Right: The original fighter triplane design was T.O.M. Sopwith's, who believed that maximum manoeuvrability could be achieved by reducing span and concentrating lift and weight far forward.

Sopwith Triplane

Nieuport Sesquiplane

Fokker D.VII

Sopwith Camel

Though only 150 of them were built, Sopwith's "Tripehounds" also proved highly successful. The five sombrely-painted machines of Naval Ten's "Black Flight" brought down 87 enemy aircraft within two months. Canadian Raymond Collishaw scored 16 of these, and later became Britain's third-ranking ace with 60 victories.

Germany's reaction to America's declaration of war was the "Amerika Programm", which called for the construction of 2,000 planes a month and a proportionate increase in engine and machine gun production. The development of a new 185 h.p. BMW engine led to a competition for a new fighter to use it, with Fokker, Albatros, Pfalz and Siemens-Schuckert all submitting designs. Lothar von Richthofen, Goering and other aces were unanimous in their praise of Fokker's D.VII, which was immediately put into mass production.

The secret of the new plane was its unusually deep aerofoil, which meant that the wings could be braced internally, eliminating drag-producing wires. This, combined with its steel-tube fuselage, gave an extremely strong structure capable of withstanding prolonged dives. Its high-lift wings and powerful engine gave it fantastic climbing ability and a ceiling of 7,700 metres, while balanced ailerons ensured manoeuvrability.

However, the greatest fighter of the war was the Sopwith Camel, responsible for downing 1,294 enemy aircraft and used by the British ace William Barker to score most of his 53 victories.

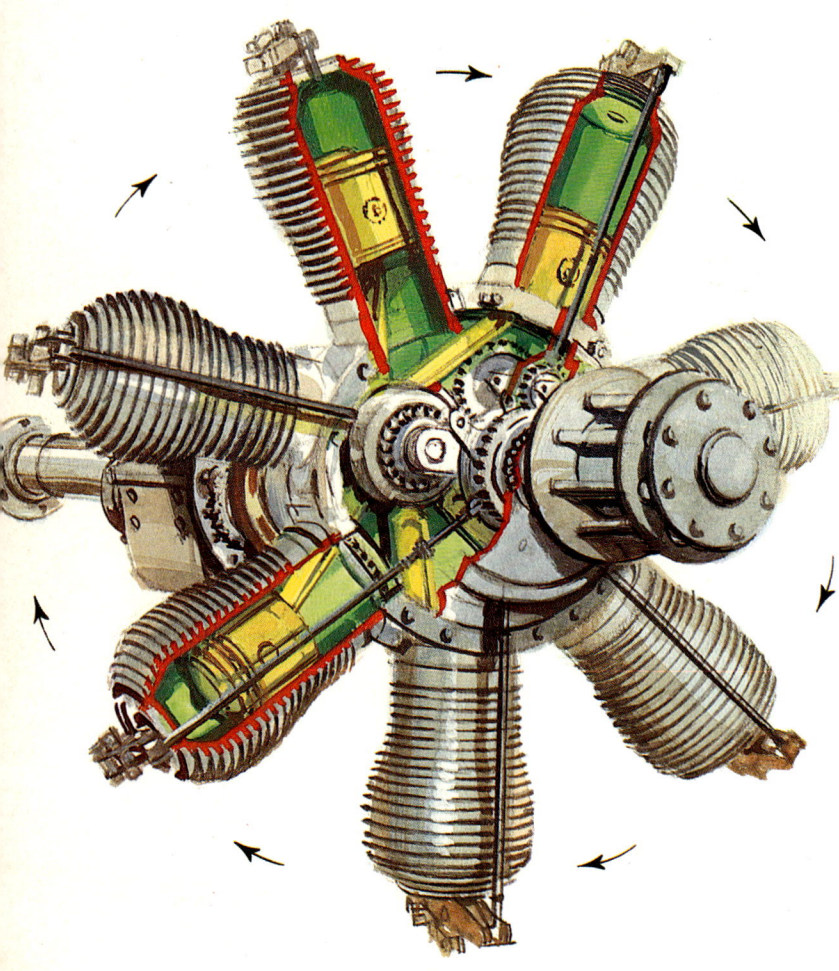

The principle of the rotary engine in which the propeller, crankcase and cylinders (seven or nine) rotate around a fixed crankshaft was originally proposed by Australian engineer Lawrence Hargrave as early as 1887, but was not successfully applied until 1909, when the French Seguin brothers produced the first 50 h.p. Gnôme rotary engine.

ducts carrying fuel, air and a lubricant (castor oil, which does not mix with gasoline) into the crankcase. Here the mixture is vaporized and forced by centrifugal pressure into the cylinders through slots which open in the pistons at the bottom of the stroke. At the top of the stroke, this explosive gas is fired by a spark-plug connected with a magneto, forcing both engine and propeller to turn. The cylinder is then cleared through a single exhaust valve (hence the name "Monosoupape", from *soupape*, French for "valve") operated by a cam and pushrod arrangement.

The rotary engine's main advantages were its relative mechanical simplicity which enabled pilots to make on-the-spot repairs when forced down, its lightness and its high power-to-weight ratio. Another asset was the gyroscopic effect created by the rotating engine, which greatly increased the manoeuvrability of such fine fighters as the Sopwith Camel and Fokker Triplane. However, rotary engines were not easy to handle, having no carburettors and only rudimentary throttles. Some, like the Rhône, could be controlled by a "blip-switch" which cut the ignition to one or more cylinders and reduced the speed from 1,250 to 900 rpm. With others, like the Gnôme, it was all or nothing at all.

The rotary's other main problem was overheating, particularly in later 9-cylinder models whose power could not be raised above 170 h.p. Development potential was thus limited, and aircraft designers turned to either in-line engines or the radial types used in the Sopwith Snipe and Salmson two-seaters.

A still greater disadvantage from the pilot's point of view was the use of castor oil as a lubricant, as the fumes had a laxative effect. Some pilots even tried to counter this by carrying bottles of milk and brandy on their patrols!

Using their pre-war racing experience, some German and Austrian car manufacturers, such as Mercedes and Daimler, had developed reliable six-cylinder, water-cooled engines which could be used in aircraft. Ranging from 80 to 120 h.p. they tended to be bulky and heavy, and their huge radiators not only impaired pilot visibility but greatly increased drag, thus slowing the plane down. Solutions to these problems were soon

Engine-power

Aircraft design and fighting performance depended ultimately on what engines were available. At first, the French and British relied heavily on rotary engines while the in-line engines built by Austrian and German car manufacturers resulted in a series of exceptional aircraft. Nevertheless, some Allied fighters, such as the SE.5 and SPAD, were based on water-cooled in-line engines, and Anton Fokker's famous "Eindecker", Triplane and D.VII were all powered by German Oberusel rotaries or by Gnômes and Le Rhônes taken from captured French machines.

In a rotary installation, the crankshaft is bolted to the airframe and is fixed. Through this shaft pass three found, however, particularly with the development of the Mercedes D.III.

In the Albatros series of fighters, for instance, the radiator, at first placed horizontally in the middle of the upper wing to reduce drag, was later offset to one side to prevent the pilot being scalded by hot water in case of a hit. The power of straight in-line engines could easily be increased by raising the compression ratio and speed of revolution, and before the end of the war Mercedes, Daimler, BMW and Hiero were producing 230 to 250 h.p. models.

Even greater power and smoother operation was obtained by placing two banks of cylinders side by side to form a V. This system was adopted by Rolls Royce for its 12-cylinder "Eagle" and for America's 400 h.p. "Liberty" engine, the most powerful built during the war. Designed in 48 hours and in mass production within a month, these engines only saw action in the American-built version of the DH.4 bomber.

One of the finest liquid-cooled designs was created by the Swiss engineer Marc Birkigt for Hispano-Suiza. Featuring monoblock aluminium cylinder heads with screwed-in steel liners, anti-friction bearings and pressure lubrication of its overhead cams, it was well ahead of its day. Weighing only 150 kg and producing 150 h.p. at 1,550 rpm, the initial version of this 90 degree V.8 formed the design basis of the SE.5 and SPAD.VII, while a later, geared version rated at 220-235 h.p. went into the SE.5a and SPAD.XIII. The gears, which raised the level of the propeller, also made it possible to install a gun between the banks of cylinders.

Italy's outstanding engine manufacturer was Isotta-Fraschini, three of whose 150 h.p. V.4s were used on the long-range Caproni bombers. This firm's 250 h.p. V.6 gave Ansaldo scouts a speed in level flight of 240 kph and the ability to climb to 4,000 metres in ten minutes, unequalled by more celebrated fighters such as the SPAD.XIII, Fokker D.VII or the Siemens-Schuckert.

Left: Engine instrumentation was limited. The SVA.5's cockpit, for example, had only a tachometer showing rpm, and gauges to indicate the oil pressure and water temperature.

The Mercedes D.III opened a new era in fighter design. A classic six-cylinder engine with overhead valves, it was initially rated at 160 h.p., but this was later raised to 180 or 185 h.p. at 1,400 rpm.

From scout to fighter

A major turning point in aerial warfare occurred in the early spring of 1915, when pre-war stunt pilot Roland Garros surprised a German Aviatik near Ostende and downed it with 25 shots from his Hotchkiss. The gun was the same as that used by Franz and Quénault, but Garros was in a single-seater and was firing *through his propeller*! The device which allowed this surprising feat consisted simply of two steel plates attached to the rear side of his propeller which deflected any shots which did not pass between the blades.

Credit for the invention of the machine gun is generally given to the Americans Hotchkiss, Maxim and Lewis who devised different methods of using a gun's recoil energy to reload and fire it automatically. The Vickers version of the Maxim design was an air-cooled, belt-fed weapon, whose chief advantage was its great firepower (up to 600 rounds per minute).

The Hotchkiss was more of an automatic rifle than a true machine gun and was consequently quite light. It was fed by a spring-loaded clip of 25 cartridges and so had to be reloaded frequently. But the most popular was the Lewis gun, the first to be mounted on a plane. Gas-operated, it was fed from a flat, horizontal, rotating drum containing 47 rounds (later 94) whose spring action drove the cartridges into the firing chamber.

Victoria Cross winner Major Lanoe Hawker was one of the first to use the Lewis, mounting it on his Bristol Scout on the left of the cockpit and angled out to clear the propeller. Later, single Lewis guns were mounted over the top wings of fighters such as the Nieuports and SE.5s. At first, pilots had to stand up in the cockpit to change magazines, but a mount was soon designed which made it possible to pivot the gun from the horizontal to the vertical. To make the most of this arrangement, the pilot had to get under his victim's tail and fire upward at an angle of 45 degrees, a manoeuvre used with great success by Albert Ball, the British ace.

Above: The deflector plates, designed jointly by Roland Garros and Saulnier, enabled the former to shoot down five enemy planes and become France's first ace.
Below: Fokker's interrupter gear proved far more effective, and resulted in the "Fokker Scourge" of 1915-16.

Lewis guns also became standard equipment for the observers in almost all Allied two-seaters: mounted on a swivelling "Scarff ring", they could cover all angles except that critical area behind and below the tail of the plane.

Yet the ultimate in fighter power came from a mistake and an accompanying stroke of genius. The mistake was made by Roland Garros, who failed to set fire to his Morane when downed behind the German lines. The stroke of genius was Anton Fokker's who, when given the French secret weapon to copy, instead produced synchronization in less than 48 hours. Whatever the gun's calibre or rate of fire, Fokker feared that bullets hitting the deflector plates would cause vibrations which would shake the engine from its mount. To replace this, he designed a cam system whereby the propeller itself would fire the gun, the bullets passing harmlessly between its blades. Using a simple mechanical linkage, he had a working model of his interrupter gear firing a Parabellum fixed to a plane of his own design and presented it to the German General Staff.

After preliminary tests at his home field at Schwerin, Fokker was ordered to take his new weapon to the front and instruct combat flyers. Legend has it that the German Crown Prince ordered him to shoot down an Allied plane to prove his invention, but the neutral Dutchman refused to fire when he had a potential victim in his sights! That honour went to Oswald Boelcke and within weeks he, Max Immelmann and the other German pilots had swept the skies of opposition: the "Fokker Scourge" had begun.

The strategic importance of synchronization was such that German pilots were forbidden to fly beyond the front, but within four months a forced landing gave the secret away to the Allies. They soon combined Fokker's linkage with Constantinesco's hydraulic system to produce their own synchronization device. The marriage of the machine gun to the fast single-seater scout was now complete, and all subsequent developments in fighter design were simply a matter of improving performance (speed, rate of climb, manoeuvrability and ceiling) and increasing firepower by adding guns or increasing their rate of fire.

1. A turning and pivoting "Scarff ring" for twin Lewis guns.
2. The "Foster mount" facilitated changing magazines in flight.
3. The angled mount used by Lanoe Hawker for his Lewis.
4. The twin, synchronized Vickers on a SPAD are within easy reach of the pilot.

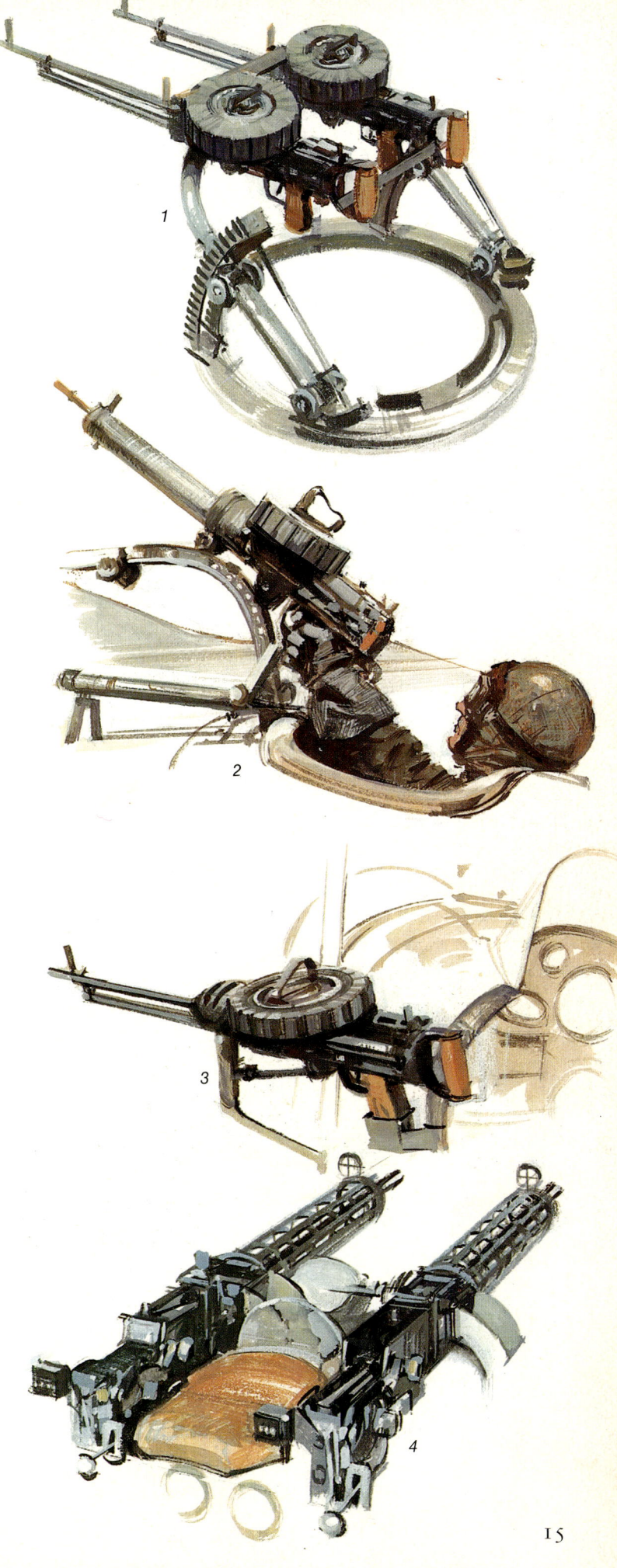

Other weapons

Machine guns were not the only weapons used by fighter pilots. Early in the war the French engineer Le Prieur developed incendiary rockets fired from tubes mounted on the outer struts of the new Nieuport fighters. Though these occasionally proved effective against captive balloons, they were soon replaced by special incendiary bullets which could be fired from standard machine guns. Rocket-assisted takeoffs were even tried, by Robert Esnault Pelterie, but the highly inflammable nature of doped fabric forbade their widespread use. Bombs of all types were more successful, and fighter pilots often flew ground support missions attacking enemy trenches, railway sidings and ammunition dumps. The first bombardments took place during the Italian conquest of Libya in 1911.

In August 1914, a lone Taube dropped a cavalry boot over Paris, warning that the German army was at its gates. A few days later another Taube, this time flown by Max Immelmann, dropped a two-kilogram bomb which narrowly missed the Sacré-Coeur but did little real damage. The first bombs weighing up to 27 kilograms were soon being launched from the wing racks of fighter aircraft all along the front.

Before all-fighter units were organized, pilots—usually in two-seaters—flew every sort of mission assigned to them, most involving photo-reconnaissance and artillery observation. Photographic missions were very important, giving warning of possible attacks. Artillery spotting was more dangerous. It involved flying low right over the front and directing fire, by radioing back to the battery where each shell fell, until the big guns were pinpointed on their targets. A simple dot-dash "clock code" was used to tell the gunners how far off target they were (for example "3-4" meant that the shell had landed at "3 o'clock" to the right of the target and 400 metres away from it). When their primitive radios failed, pilots had to swoop low over the battery and drop messages in containers trailing pennants. Danger came not only from anti-aircraft fire on both sides of the front but also from enemy fighters and even from the shells which the observers were guiding!

Early cameras were ungainly, single-plate models which the observer had to hold steady against the buffeting of the slipstream, but they brought back useful information.

Bomb rack

Artillery shell

Aerial bombs

Flêchettes

Far right: Another anti-personnel weapon was the flêchette, a small, pointed dart dropped in large numbers from canisters on to troops.

Flêchettes, too, proved inadequate, but became popular with British pilots, who used them for nightly dart games in the mess.

17

The making of a pilot

Pilots were as rare as aircraft when the war broke out, and the few flying schools were generally run by manufacturers as a way of advertising their planes. The army therefore had to build its own schools and recruit potential aces.

Who were these young adventurers in whom the warring powers placed their hopes? Some, like Guynemer and Ball, were boys fresh from school, barely able to join without their parents' permission. Others, like Nungesser and Lufbery, were seasoned soldiers of fortune who had already seen much of the world but returned hurriedly to their native land when they saw it was in danger. Many were cavalry officers who transferred to the air arm when it became clear that horses were of little use in modern warfare. Among these were von Richthofen, Baracca and the first man to weld together an integrated fighter squadron, Tricornot de Rose.

America's Rickenbacker had been a racing driver and General Pershing's private chauffeur before being admitted to the air service, while Georges Boillot had competed in the last Grand Prix before the war. Still another member of the élite, balloon-busting "Sportifs" squadron was Maurice Boyau, who had captained France's international rugby team. But, whatever their past history, they all had to submit to the same procedure after signing up—interminable waiting in line

Left: As the value of aircraft soon became clear to the military, new flying fields were built, and growing numbers of young men were recruited.

Above: Future pilots began their training in the classroom, studying the theory of flight and aircraft design, before actually learning to fly.

for physicals, for uniforms, for food, and the inevitable, fussy dress-parades and drill.

It was vital for these potential pilots to understand how the vacuum created by the airflow over the curved top surface of a wing caused a lifting force which enabled a plane to fly, and why below a certain speed this lift was lost and a plane stalled.

They had to learn the structure and purpose of all parts of a plane—the wings, fuselage, empennage (tail surfaces), landing gear, engine and, above all, the control surfaces which a pilot used to manoeuvre his craft: the vertical stabilizer and rudder for directional motion, the horizontal stabilizer and elevators for vertical movement and the ailerons which enabled him to bank and turn and avoid skidding.

Another important aspect of ground school was a course in engine mechanics. Though many recruits were familiar with motorcycle or car engines, those of aircraft were different in many respects and a pilot had to know them really well to be able to make emergency repairs in case of a forced landing. This entailed many hours of practical work, stripping down and reassembling engines, learning the intricacies of a carburettor and tracing the ignition from the magneto via the brushes to the spark-plugs.

Meteorology and navigation were also taught, as a pilot had to be able to judge the weather and avoid bad conditions when necessary. Learning dead reckoning and navigating a plane over clouds using only a compass, air speed, drift and elapsed time saved many a pilot from becoming hopelessly lost or being forced to land behind the enemy lines because of lack of fuel. Only after he had mastered all of these disciplines was a fledgling pilot allowed to begin real flight training.

From theory to practice

There were two entirely different schools of thought on how a pilot should be trained. The British and Germans generally favoured the dual control method of teaching a pilot how to *fly* a plane while the French and Italians basically initiated their fledglings in how to *drive* one.

Under the "système Blériot", as taught in Italy's two major flying schools at Avieno and Centocelle, students were immediately put at the controls of a single-seater "Pingouin", an old Blériot monoplane whose wings had been clipped to half their span so that it could taxi but not take off. After queuing for his turn, the student was given brief instructions by the head instructor, the chocks were pulled away from the wheels, and he was on his own, trying to keep the plane on a straight course as it bumped and skidded across the field. Classes were usually so crowded that each student could make only a few such runs a day, particularly as instruction was restricted to 4—8 a.m. and 4—8 p.m., wind conditions being considered too perilous during the rest of the day.

Two weeks of this exercise might be needed before the student moved on to the next stage on a "Rouleur". This was a slightly more powerful Blériot (70 h.p. instead of 50 h.p.) with full-span wings, but the student still had to keep it on the ground. This stage was intended to give the young pilot enough self-confidence to stop him panicking when he finally graduated to a "Décolleur", an 80 h.p. version of the same machine. As its name implies (*décoller* = "to take off" in French), this plane could actually fly, and the pilot would first rise to the dizzy height of 3 metres, gradually working up to 8, 15 or even 30 metres—all in a straight line! Only then, and only if he had not ground-looped or otherwise damaged the craft, was the student given instructions in how to make a turn and perform stunts such as spirals. Only 40 per cent of the beginners got through this stage!

In order to earn the coveted brevet of the fighter pilot two tough tests then had to be passed. First came an endurance flight of one hour at an altitude of over 1,800 metres, not an easy feat for the chilled pilot in an open cockpit, as the unstable Blériot had to be handled very skilfully at this height, and shifting winds or storms could cause disaster. The second test was a 250-kilometre cross-country flight with two stops to refuel and sign a register. Emergency landings were frequent, and the trainee airman had to apply all the knowledge he had acquired in ground school—navigation, meteorology and, above all, mechanics—if he wanted to succeed.

Not all became fighter pilots, of course. Many more were needed for observation, reconnaissance and bombing work, and even such top-scoring aces as von Richthofen, Billy Bishop and Silvio Scaroni started in two-seaters. Within six weeks of being posted to the front as a fighter pilot Scaroni downed three Austrian bombers during one patrol, the first Italian to achieve a triple. He later repeated this feat. His final score of 26 victories made him Italy's second ace and a holder of the rarely-awarded *Medaglia d'Oro al Valore Militare*.

Below left: Inexperienced pilots landing in a cross-wind frequently found themselves spinning like tops. Despite the Blériot's ruggedness, landing gear and wingtips suffered from this treatment, and many beginners were "washed-out" as a result of these ground-loops.

Aerial gunnery

A fighter pilot's training had nine different phases, and learning to handle a wing-warping Blériot or Caudron was just the beginning. Student pilots then graduated to real fighters such as the Nieuport "Bébé" or N.17. This was a crucial stage, for pilots who were clever, resourceful and well-coordinated went on to gunnery school, while those who had frequent accidents or poor reflexes were relegated to bombing, artillery spotting or photo–reconnaissance machines, all involving danger without glory.

French gunnery training was centred at Cazaux, by a lake near the southern resort town of Arcachon, a thinly populated area where falling bullets would do little harm. Pilots first had to learn the intricacies of the Lewis and Vickers machine guns and their synchronizing gear, dismantling and reassembling them on the ground and discovering how to cure a "jam". This was usually caused by an ill-fitting cartridge sticking in the breech, and a pilot's life often depended on how quickly he could clear his gun and be ready to return to the attack. It was easy enough to clear a jam on the ground, but once airborne, the Lewis mounted over the wing of a Nieuport had to be pulled back on its hinged mount and its magazine changed using both hands and letting go of the joystick. The twin Vickers on the later SPADs gave fewer problems: it was unusual for both to jam at once, and in any case their breeches came back into the cockpit where a sharp blow with a hammer normally cleared the jam.

Aircraft design and development

Fokker
"Eindecker"

Speed, manoeuvrability and firepower were the three essential characteristics of a fighter and so were avidly sought by the warring powers. Captured enemy planes in good condition were immediately tested by ace pilots. Any good points were then noted and incorporated into a new generation of combat aircraft. Even Fokker's famous "Eindecker" was based on a captured French Morane monoplane which the Dutch designer dismantled and copied. Better flight characteristics were achieved mainly through adding ribs to the wing structure, thus improving airflow: however, no change was made to the old system of wing-warping. The resulting tangle of drag-producing wires combined with its low-powered engine to make the plane slow and completely unmanoeuvrable at high altitudes.

The E.1's forward firing machine gun gave it a formidable reputation as the "Fokker Scourge", but by early 1916 it had been outclassed by such British pushers as the DH.2 and FE.2 and, above all, by the nippy French Nieuport series. The "Bébé" Nieuport 11 and its successor the N.17 were sesquiplanes: their upper full-span, twin spar wings were connected to a narrow lower pair by a V-shaped strut. This arrangement was designed to combine the rigidity and high lift of a trussed biplane design with the good visibility and low drag of the monoplane.

The Nieuport was originally armed with only a single Lewis gun over the top wing, but a synchronized Vickers was added later. With it, the Allies were able to regain mastery of the air in 1916, and it was the plane in which aces such as Bishop, Ball, Baracca, Nungesser and Guynemer won their spurs.

The advantages of the sesquiplane were quickly seen by German designers: Albatros modified their plywood-fuselaged D.I and D.II accordingly to produce the D.III and D.V models, used by the "Circuses" until replaced by the even more gaudily painted Fokker Triplanes and the rugged D.VII.

reconnoitred the Zeppelin factory at Friedrichshafen, rowing across Lake Constance after making his way through Switzerland incognito. Returning to his base in Belfort, he and his men took off in three Avro 504s and successfully followed a carefully mapped-out course avoiding neutral territory via Mulhouse and across the Black Forest to Schaffhausen before turning south toward Lake Constance.

It soon became clear that denying the skies to enemy planes was vitally important and that this could not be done with unarmed aircraft. At first pilots used their sidearms and rifles to fire at each other, but when Gabriel Voisin mounted an infantry machine gun on one of his pushers the fighter was born.

On 5th October 1914, not far from Reims, Franz and Quénault spotted an Aviatik two-seater headed for home. Quénault fired two clips from the tripod over his pilot's head before his Hotchkiss jammed. The German plane spiralled to the ground, the first victim in the history of aerial combat. As well as medals, Franz and Quénault were rewarded with their victim's engine, the sale of which provided delicacies for their mess for the next two months!

Below: Dipping to within three metres of the water to avoid detection, they then soared to 400 metres before diving on the well-defended Zeppelin factory and gasworks. The result was a tremendous explosion and flames leaping high into the air.

A new weapon takes off

Despite General Foch's pre-war statement that airplanes were mere playthings, they soon proved their usefulness as the army's "eyes". It was British pilots who spotted the gap in the German lines near Mons which enabled their troops to close ranks with the French.

During the first four days of September, flights of French reconnaissance planes scoured the countryside to the north and west of Paris, rushing back to General Gallieni's headquarters to report the enemy's position. One pilot after another reported no troops west of the Oise river and that the entire right wing of the German army seemed to be swerving eastward. Relying on this information, Gallieni sent his taxi-riding garrison in that direction. On the evening of the 4th General Joffre informed his staff: "Gentlemen, we will fight on the Marne." Within ten days the Kaiser's push had come to a halt; Paris (and France) were saved. Thus the first victory on the Marne owed much to the pilots and observers in their Blériots, Voisins, Caudrons and Farmans.

Considering the limited range of the light and fragile aircraft available, it no wonder that the Allied General Staff saw them as passive observers, their fears focused on Imperial Germany's impressive fleet of Zeppelins. Then, within ten days of the outbreak of war, the French successfully bombed the Zeppelin shed at Metz. Shortly afterwards British Lieutenant Marix, flying a Sopwith Tabloid, bombed and completely destroyed the newly commissioned Z.XIX.

Lieutenant Rumney Samson of the Royal Navy achieved a still more impressive feat when he personally the Marne, trapping a large contingent of French troops who tried to escape in the direction of the Aisne and Verdun. The German advance was accompanied by a squadron of Aviatik observation planes. Lieutenant Gironde of the 16th Dragoons learned from a peasant that there was a German air unit based at Vivières, just north of Villers Cotterêts, and decided to attack it.

In the dead of night, he dismounted half his troop only a few hundred metres from the Germans and sent them ahead to clear the way. They crawled into range, struck down a sentry and set fire to a truck, lighting the way for the charge. Sabre raised and leading his platoon of lancers at full gallop toward the planes, Gironde was met by a deadly hail of bullets from a machine gun mounted on the German staff car. Within seconds the field was strewn with the writhing bodies of dead or wounded horses and dragoons. Nevertheless, the attack had achieved its goal of destroying the enemy planes, and had given Gironde the distinction of leading one of the last cavalry charges in history.

The weapon which made air combat possible spelled doom to the cavalry, whose twin missions of observation and pursuit were soon in the hands of the airmen. By this time former cavalrymen, such as von Richthofen, Nungesser and Baracca, had become pilots and aces—the new ''Knights of the Air''!

Affectionately known as a "chicken coop" because of its many wires and struts, the Caudron G.3 was the mainstay of the French air force, widely used for observation, photo-reconnaissance and light bombing as well as for towing targets at gunnery school.

Practice in marksmanship also started on the ground, the pilots shooting skeet or firing rifles at rising balloons; they also took turns firing at stationary targets from a rail-mounted cab or fast-moving steam launch. Next they were given planes with live ammunition and, at 3,000 metres, released weighted parachutes at which they then fired.

Later exercises included strafing ground targets along the Atlantic shore, and finally shooting at a sleeve target towed by a Caudron. Aiming through the ring-sight on the front of the fuselage the future ace had to determine angle of approach and range in a simulated fighter attack and spray the drogue with as many shots as possible. The score was determined by the ratio of ammunition used to the number of holes in the sleeve, and real marksmen soon graduated and were sent to the front. Camera guns were also used, to simulate dog-fights and give practice in tactics.

Preparing for combat

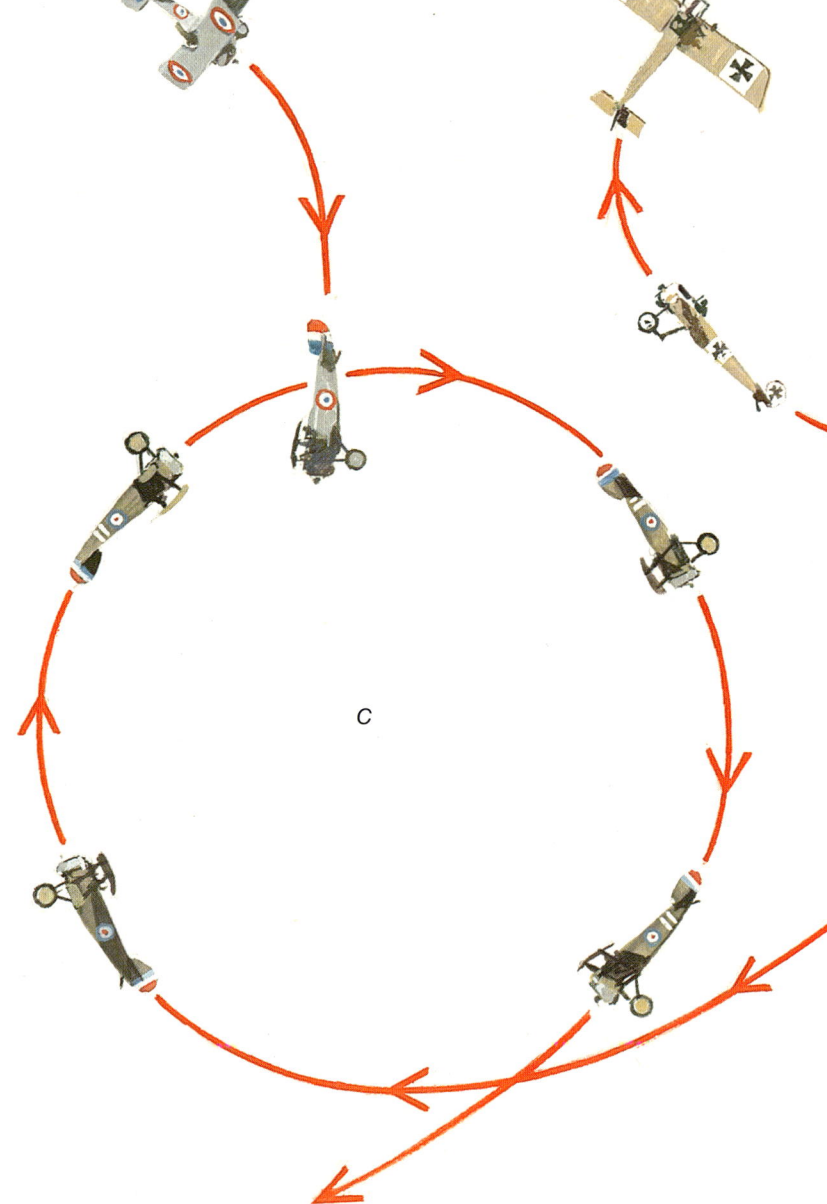

Having mastered gunnery, the pilot went to advanced flying school where he learned the manoeuvres which could save his life. First came basic acrobatics—loops and slow rolls—then the two were combined to give the "split S", or the "Immelmann turn" (invented by the German ace to reverse his direction after an attack and again be in a position from which to dive down on his foe). The "falling leaf" (slide-slipping in alternate directions) was an invaluable manoeuvre, and many pilots escaped by spinning downwards as if hit and then pulling out to race for home.

Another popular tactic when faced with superior numbers was to form a "Lufbery circle", a sort of aerial roundabout in which one plane's guns would protect another should an enemy get too close under his tail, and from which the sky could be surveyed in comparative safety. This implied the ability to fly in formation and to work as part of a team. Ambitious pilots wishing to raise their score could of course fly solo on volunteer patrols, but the bulk of the squadron's work was done in formations of from 3 to 12 aircraft.

First, a pilot had to learn how to join a formation, cutting inside his flight leader's path to get ever closer and take up his assigned position. He needed the ability not only to judge distances accurately but also to co-ordinate his movements with those of others and keep alert at all times to avoid collisions. Maintaining a constant position between two fast-moving, unstable fighters is not easy when flying straight and level; it is even more difficult when climbing, diving, turning or executing more complicated manoeuvres. Wingmen also had to learn their leader's signals: hand signals indicating a change of direction or of tactics, and the

wing-waggling which meant "Prepare to attack!"

Some selected pilots were also trained in night flying as cities or other installations sometimes had to be defended against bombers or Zeppelins. There was much to learn in a hurry; heavy losses at the front meant that many British pilots arrived in France with only 20 hours' solo flying time!

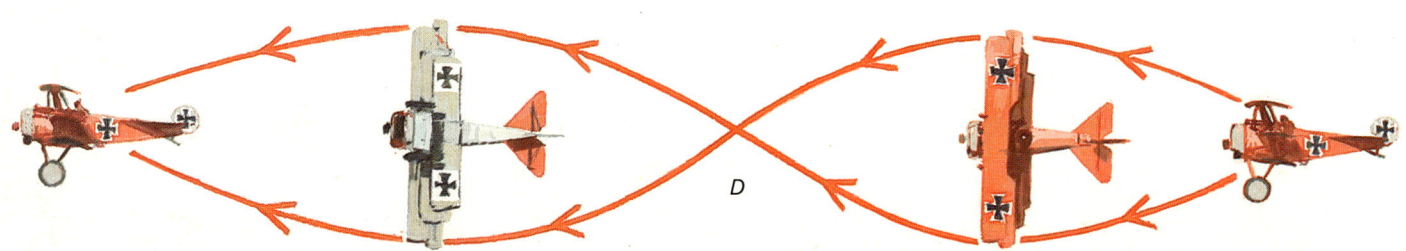

B

Some basic manoeuvres: A—*the split S*—rolling the plane into an inverted position and then pulling it into a vertical dive. B—*the Immelmann turn*—doing a half-loop and then rolling out at the top. C—*the loop*—unless smooth, the plane tends to stall out at the top or lose its wings coming out. D—*the slow roll*—not as easy as it looks, since the controls are crossed and reversed when upside down. Requires considerable coordination.

Ferrying and other duties

The new pilots were not all sent straight to the front, and while awaiting assignment to a fighter squadron were often asked to deliver new planes from the factory to the front line. Pilots were expected to be able to fly any kind of aircraft after only a few hours' practice, and ferrying was a test of their navigational skills. In France and Germany where the terrain was generally flat and criss-crossed by many roads, railways and canals this raised few problems. In Austria, however, it meant flying long distances over the rugged Carpathians to the Eastern Front or south over the forbidding Alps to the Italian sector.

The air war was not confined to the Western Front, running from Belgium to Switzerland, or to the shorter but equally active Italian Front, where Italian pilots aided by squadrons of British Camels and French SPADs battled Austrian "Fliks" *(Flieger-kompagnien)* and *Jagdstaffeln* flown in from Germany. In the north, on an even longer front stretching from the Baltic to the Black Sea, Russian airmen flew licence-built Nieuports and Moranes or Sikorski's fighters and giant bombers (the first four-engined aircraft). Strafing and bombing railway depots far behind the lines, they had to fight off patrols of Brandenberg Starstrutters or speedy and manoeuvrable Phoenix fighters bearing the black Iron Cross of the Austrian Empire.

Russia's air force also had a score of aces, including ex-cavalryman Alexander Kazakov who always flew

1. Personal insignia of Austrian ace Sandor Kaszka.
2. That of Russian Captain Krulen.
3. That of Russia's top ace, Captain Kazakov.
4. Insignia of Russia's first fighter group.

Below: A typical reconnaissance plane, the Halberstadt C.V was a two-seater with a fixed camera shooting through a gap in the fuselage. These aircraft were mass-produced by Aviatik, BFW and DFW, as well as by Halberstädter Flugzeugwerke. The C.VII model had a ceiling of nearly 9,000 metres, making it almost unassailable, despite its slow speed.

3

4

with an icon of St Nicholas in his cockpit and was officially credited with 17 victories though his real score was at least 30. Another Alexander, de Seversky, valiantly fought on after his leg had been blown off. He emigrated to America after the war, where he developed one of the greatest of the World War II fighters, the P.47 Thunderbolt. Sikorski also went to America, and produced the flying boats which opened up the great transoceanic air routes as well as developing the first practical helicopter.

The top Austrian aces included Godwin Brumowski (40 victories) and Frank Linke-Crawford, whose epic battle with William Barker over Italy is still celebrated in RAF messes.

The fighting unit

Training complete, the new pilots eagerly awaited being posted to the front. Only as members of a fighting unit, whether *Jasta*, squadron, *escadrille* or *squadriglia*, could they test their acquired skills, fly the most advanced planes available and become aces like their heroes. Before the battle of Verdun, most single-seater scouts had simply been attached to general purpose squadrons, but during the "Fokker Scourge" the French formed the first élite all-fighter *Escadrille de Chasse* equipped with the Nieuport "Bébé". Almost simultaneously, Britain's 24 Squadron under Lanoe Hawker flew its new DH.2 pushers into France.

Though equipped with faster and more manoeuvrable aircraft, it was mainly the fact that they fought as units that made these formations successful. Realizing this, the German high command soon reorganized the Imperial Air Force into 14-plane *Jagdstaffeln* or "hunting packs", abbreviated to *Jasta*. The first of these, *Jasta 2*, was put into the hands of Oswald Boelcke who, with Max Immelmann, had helped to sweep the skies of northern France clear of Allied aircraft, earning Germany's highest distinction, the *Pour le Mérite* or Blue Max. An ace with 40 planes to his credit, Boelcke was also a theoretician, a superb organizer and a leader who hand-picked and trained his men.

His new command was completely independent; with its own transport, fuel supplies, ground crews, armourers and medical facilities, it could be moved to any part of the front. Realizing the importance of morale to a pilot's fighting ability, Boelcke quartered his officers in luxurious French châteaux and his crews in nearby villages, allowing them plenty of time off. He also suggested that the pilots should paint their personal insignia on the fuselages of their planes. The gaudy colours the pilots chose, and the tents used as hangars, caused the nickname of "Circus" to be given to the later, larger groups. These units, comprising four *Jastas*, were known as *Jagdgeschwader*, or JG, and could send up 56 fighters at a time.

With their colourful paintwork, tent hangars and independent transport, the *Jagdgeschwader* naturally became known as "Circuses". Renamed *Jasta Boelcke* after the ace's death, *Jasta 2* reaped a heavy toll of Allied aircraft under von Richthofen (the Red Baron) and his successors.

Dawn patrol

Once at the front, the new fighter pilot quickly found that his main function was to fly patrols, attacking any enemy planes that might try to cross the lines to observe, bomb or strafe, or any that could be pursued into enemy territory. Each squadron was usually required to fly three two-and-a-half hour patrols a day. With four squadrons to a pursuit group, constant air cover could be provided from dawn until dusk.

Dawn patrols over northern France meant getting up at 3.30 or 4 a.m., snatching a hurried breakfast, donning flight gear and being on the flight line by 5 a.m. The mechanics too had been up for hours, checking over the planes and warming them up, then standing by to pull away the chocks.

Some American squadron insignia:
1. The executioner of the 25th Aero Squadron.
2. The "hat in the ring" of the 94th Aero Squadron, symbolizing the entry of the USA into the battle-arena.
3. The Sioux's head of the *Lafayette Escadrille*.
4. The eagle of the 27th Aero Squadron, to which "balloon-buster" Frank Luke belonged.

1

The first and all-American dawn patrol was flown by the Nieuport 28s of the "hat-in-the-ring" 94th Aero Squadron commanded by Major Raoul Lufbery. A veteran of the famous *Lafayette Escadrille*, "Luf" already had 17 victories to his credit and a well-merited collection of French and British decorations. Choosing beginners Eddie Rickenbacker and Douglas Campbell to accompany him, Lufbery warned them to keep their eyes open, stay close and head for home if trouble developed. They took off at dawn and flew towards the front at 4,000 metres. Shell-pitted no-man's-land with its zig-zag of trenches was easily distinguished even at that height, and was made even more obvious by the white puffs, sudden explosions and whistling noise of shrapnel from German anti-aircraft batteries.

Back at the base Lufbery asked his fledglings if they had seen any other planes. Receiving only blank stares in reply he told them that five SPADs had crossed their path, that four Albatroses were several kilometres ahead of them and that a Rumpler observation two-seater surveyed them from a vantage point 300 metres above.

This was the veteran's lesson for the beginner: "Look and live!"

A few days later, the operations telephone rang to report an approaching Albatros, escorted by a Pfalz fighter. Campbell and Alan Winslow immediately took off and within a few minutes had shot both down within 500 metres of their own hangars. American victories followed swiftly, despite the Nieuport's tendency to shed its upper wing fabric in a dive, and Douglas Campbell became America's first ace.

The greatest American ace was to be Eddie Rickenbacker, a pre-war racing driver who took command of the 94th after Lufbery's fall in flames and welded it into a first-class fighting unit, replacing the dangerous and obsolete Nieuports with sturdy SPADs. A top mechanic as well as a thorough, inspired flight leader, "Rick" saw to it that his pilots were well-trained, his planes and guns in top condition and his squadron's tactics appropriate to the job, whether strafing trenches, flying patrols or attacking balloons. His 26 victories earned him the Congressional Medal of Honour.

2

3

4

Pour le Mérite (Blue Max)

Iron Cross

Personal gear

Warm clothing was essential for all pilots. At first, altitudes of over 3,000 metres were rare, but increased engine power and improved aircraft design meant that pilots were soon flying two-and-a-half-hour missions at between 4,500 and 6,000 metres, where temperatures were well below zero even in summer. It was not until late in the war that the various air forces issued regulation equipment, and pilots could wear anything.

Over their uniform tunics, for if forced down they had to prove their rank and military status, most pilots wore a short flying jacket or full-length greatcoat, sometimes woollen but more often fur-lined leather. Some, like Britain's Lanoe Hawker, sported a splendid fox-fur jacket, while others, like Jean Navarre, favoured a sturdy canvas coat with a fur collar. Navarre added another individual touch by wearing a lady's bright red silk stocking instead of a helmet! Less garish and more popular, however, was the "passe-montagne" or Balaclava helmet. This was usually topped by a leather flying helmet and a pair of goggles to protect the pilot's

The Red Baron, Manfred von Richthofen, always wore his decorations when flying, the Blue Max dangling from his neck and the Iron Cross pinned to the left breast of his tunic.

The observer

Artillery spotting and photo-reconnaissance were probably the most dangerous of a pilot's duties, being performed in slow two-seaters. The observer in the rear cockpit not only had to ward off enemy fighters with his ring-mounted machine guns but also had to radio back to the battery the exact location of where each shell landed. This meant flying low over the trenches through a constant barrage of anti-aircraft fire. Furthermore, as the ideal altitude for such scouting was the same as the top of the trajectory of a howitzer shell, many pilots had the awesome experience of seeing a huge shell

The Biff was an exceptional machine, speedy (196 kph), manoeuvrable and with a sting in both nose and tail. It could be handled like a single-seater and the closeness of its two cockpits ensured good team work between pilot and observer.

tumbling toward them before falling slowly on to the enemy lines. Some planes were even brought down by their own artillery because of this!

Short-range photographic missions were equally perilous as planes had to fly straight and level for minutes at a time to get the series of overlapping photographs needed by army headquarters. Long-range missions involved navigational problems and, of course, the danger of engine failure deep in enemy territory or, on the Italian Front, in the forbidding Alps.

Italian airmen faced increasing difficulties late in 1917 when German squadrons were sent south in support of the Austrians during the Caporetto offensive. After withdrawing to the Piave, they themselves received help from the north in the form of French units flying SPADs and Nieuports and a British wing equipped with Camels and Bristol Fighters, known as "Biffs".

Biffs were speedy, manoeuvrable two-seaters, and William Barker's 139 Squadron of the RAF performed wonders with them on the Italian Front in support of the SPADs and Hanriots of Baracca's equally famous *91 Squadriglia*. Like many aces, Francesco Baracca was a cavalry officer before training as a pilot. Late in 1916, Baracca scored his fifth victory and became an ace; it was then that he had his crest, a black horse, painted on the side of his Nieuport 17. He flew escort with fellow aces Piccio and Baracchini on long-range bombing missions over Trieste and other Austrian bases, and when the SPAD. XIII became available in Italy upped his score to 34 victories with a series of amazing doubles.

Unharmed in all his aerial combats, Baracca finally fell to ground fire during a strafing mission over the Austrian trenches in June 1918. Ten years later, his widow gave Enzio Ferrari permission to use his crest and racing cars have borne it ever since!

Pilots found little satisfaction in strafing trenches, considering ground troops unworthy opponents. Many of them were ex-cavalrymen and reluctant to fire at the horses still used to haul artillery. However, ground-fire from rifles and machine guns downed large numbers of planes.

Self-powered AA gun

Anti-aircraft machine gun

Stump-mounted "French 75"

Tactical missions

Army headquarters quickly realized that aircraft could be used as airborne artillery, and during major offensives single-seater fighter units were pressed into tactical service. Most fighter pilots disliked strafing trenches or engaging in other low-level missions against troops as they considered the battle unfair. An exception to this was the strafing of enemy airfields, and RFC Squadrons 56 and 100 relished visiting Circus bases, bombing hangars and shooting planes as they tried to take off to defend their field. Such raids invariably brought reprisals, and von Richthofen himself led strikes against British and French bases.

Other targets for low-level attacks included railway sidings, farmhouses being used as headquarters, ammunition dumps spotted by aerial photography and enemy troop concentrations on the move toward the front. Pilots were assigned specific targets during such missions and, their planes weighed down by four bombs in addition to their usual guns and ammunition, threaded their way past fighter patrols and enemy anti-aircraft fire to roar in on their targets at less than 60 metres, repeating the run as many times as necessary. Anti-aircraft guns were a serious threat at such low altitudes and, though initially they consisted of ordinary field guns like the "French 75" mounted on tree stumps so that they could fire up at an angle, self-powered rapid-fire guns were developed later, on mobile mounts which could be moved quickly from one part of the front to another. Machine guns were still the greatest danger, however, and some pilots on strafing missions also fell to the concentrated rifle fire of troops in the trenches.

Every German *Jagdstaffel* was thrown into the battle during the great spring offensive of 1918, and in September 1918 Billy Mitchell had 1,481 planes under his command to help the French and American armies reduce the Saint Mihiel salient. Sending 400-plane attack brigades to alternate sides of the bulge, he kept the German air forces off balance and was thus able to use his bombers to strike at enemy communications and troop concentrations in the rear. Using his planes like cavalry units, Mitchell proved that an intelligently used air arm could destroy not only an army's ability to fight but also its morale.

1st victory

The marksman

Like Canada's highest scoring ace Billy Bishop (72 confirmed victories) and Germany's Manfred von Richthofen (80 victories), René Fonck had a hard time getting started. A navigational error during a cross-country flight almost caused him to fail his pilot's training and he was subsequently assigned to clumsy two-seaters doing bombing and reconnaissance work. Yet even at this stage of his career he revealed the marksmanship that eventually made him the Allied Ace of aces when, flying a cumbersome Caudron G. IV, he managed to shoot down two German aircraft. This brought him his first citation and a transfer to the legendary *Cigognes* fighter group, which had recently been equipped with the new SPAD.XIII.

The SPAD's high aspect ratio required additional struts halfway along its span, which made it exceptionally strong and above all stable, an ideal gun platform for the twin Vickers mounted just in front of the cockpit. Fonck scored his first victory as a *Cigogne* on 3rd May 1917 and by the following February had 26 enemy planes to his credit, second only to Nungesser (Guynemer having fallen in September). After scoring three doubles in March and April 1918, on 9th May he successfully shot down three planes in a 45-second fight, the wreckage of all three falling within a circle of 400 metres. Later that same afternoon, he brought down still another two-seater and two of the Fokkers and Albatroses which had come to its rescue. This won him the *Croix d'Officier de la Légion d'Honneur*.

Fonck had another fantastic day of fighting late in September, attacking five Fokkers and sending two of them down in flames before chasing and shooting down a German reconnaissance plane during the same patrol. On another patrol that day, he and three squadron-mates, Fontaine, Loup and Brugère, were attacked by eight Fokkers, reinforced mid-battle by five Albatroses. The fight was long, but Fonck downed two of the Fokkers and one Albatros, raising his score to 68.

The secret of Fonck's success was his marksmanship, and he constantly practised deflection shooting when on the ground and planned his battles in minute detail. So accurate was his aim that it frequently took him no more than five or six rounds to make a kill and, had the Vickers on his SPAD not jammed from time to time, his ultimate score might have been well above the 75 victories with which he is officially credited.

2nd victory

3rd victory
(a few seconds later)

A cautious yet fearless pilot, Fonck once attacked a formation of three enemy planes head-on and downed the trio in ten seconds, each receiving one brief burst.

Like its forerunner, the SPAD.VII, the Béchereau-designed SPAD.XIII used a Hispano-Suiza V.8 220 h.p. engine (later 235 h.p.), which gave it a speed and climbing power unequalled by other fighters of the time (215 kph and over 460 revolutions per minute).

Voluntary patrols

Guynemer's gun was mounted between the banks of a 200 h.p. Hispano-Suiza, whose gearing allowed it to be fired through the propeller hub.

Even more determined to down his country's enemies was France's legendary air hero, Georges Guynemer, who, having won every possible medal, stated that his ultimate decoration would be the "wooden cross". Rejected because of his frail health, he pestered the authorities until they allowed him to become a mechanic then insisted further so that he could take flight training. Downing his first plane from a two-seater Morane in 1915, he followed this with more victories and was assigned to the élite *Cigogne* group.

Because of his position as France's leading ace, Guynemer had three planes at his disposal, all nicknamed "Vieux Charles". One was a standard model which he used during his squadron's regular patrols, the second a high-compression type adapted for high-altitude flights and the third a version made specially for him and delivered from the factory with a two-kilogram gun in its nose as well as a tracer-firing machine gun. This he saved for his voluntary patrols, the solitary flights he customarily made after the squadron's regular work was done. Alone in the freezing air at 6,000 metres, he would wait for an enemy formation to pass below then flip his SPAD into a vertical dive out of the sun, carefully choosing his victim and adjusting his aim with a stream of tracers before opening fire. Then, ploughing

The stork, symbol of German-occupied Alsace, was used as an insignia by France's élite fighter groups. This version was painted on the fuselages of Guynemer's squadron.

through the formation of Fokkers and Albatroses, he would soar upward to attack again—and again!

So persistent was Guynemer in flying whenever the weather permitted that during one two-month period he engaged in 388 combats, shooting down 36 planes and 3 balloons and forcing another 36 enemy aircraft to land. Though he himself was shot down and wounded seven times, nothing could keep him from the front; once, hardly recovered from his wounds, he coolly allowed an enemy gunner to empty his entire 500-round magazine at him without firing a shot in return—just to prove he still had the courage to continue in combat!

On another occasion, after an inconclusive fight with German ace Ernst Udet during which the latter had exhausted his ammunition, Guynemer simply saluted his foe for his skill and courage and flew home to renew the duel another day. However, the gruelling pace of Guynemer's fighting eventually told on his nerves and, on September 11 1917 he disappeared in combat over Poelcapelle. Instead of his coveted wooden cross, a grateful France erected a monument to him in the Pantheon.

The pilot's best friends

The pilot's best friends were his mechanics and the other members of his ground crew. At least six to eight highly skilled men were needed to keep a pilot flying and fighting, for he rarely returned completely unscathed and there were always bullet or shrapnel holes

to be patched, broken rigging wires or bent propellers to be replaced, guns to be oiled and reloaded and engines to be overhauled. Riggers mended the control cables and the wires which kept the wings at the proper angle to the fuselage, while other specialists repaired fabric, broken struts and longerons, and replaced shock cords stretched by rough landings. Ground crews had to work from well before dawn until well after sunset.

Nungesser, Guynemer and Rickenbacker had all been top mechanics before training as pilots and were well aware of the value of a good grease-monkey, such as Pochon. He became Nungesser's best friend, accompanying him on his frequent leaves to Paris, nursing the ace's SPAD and even helping to lift "the Indestructible" into his cockpit when he decided to ignore both his superior's orders and his doctor's advice. Nungesser was inconsolable when, after a night on the town, the car in which he and Pochon were returning overturned and the mechanic was killed.

Hospitalized time and again because of his injuries, Nungesser was often helped from his crutches into the cockpit so that he could continue fighting, despite his doctor's objections.

Balloon-busting

British gasbags, German *Drachen* and French *saucisses* were all balloons anchored to the ground and used for the same vital purpose—observation. Observers equipped with field glasses, telephones and parachutes sat in wicker gondolas slung beneath the bags and reported on troop movements and the accuracy of the artillery fire. Spaced at intervals of about six kilometres all along the front, these balloons could be winched down in a matter of minutes. Far from being sitting ducks for enterprising pilots, they were heavily defended by machine gun nests on the ground and high-flying fighter patrols above. The credit for downing a balloon was the same as for any other enemy aircraft, and many pilots concentrated on this dangerous game.

French aces Boyau and Coiffard specialized in setting *Drachen* aflame, as did Britain's Anthony Beauchamp-Proctor, while *Jasta 15*'s commander Heinrich Gontermann downed 18 Allied balloons to raise his final score to 39. America's leading balloon-buster was Frank Luke, who in his brief 17-day career of combat flying managed to destroy 21 of them. Skidding and weaving out of the sunset to avoid ground fire, Luke was protected from above during his low-level incendiary attacks by squadron-mate Joseph Wehner who never hesitated to fight off up to eight attacking Fokkers singlehanded.

Belgium's top ace Willy Coppens de Houthulst failed on his first attempt due to a shortage of incendiary bullets, but after begging the required ammunition from a neighbouring British squadron soon became the best of them all, downing enemy balloons as fast as they were raised and enthusiastically celebrating each victory by throwing his agile Hanriot fighter into an incredible display of acrobatics.

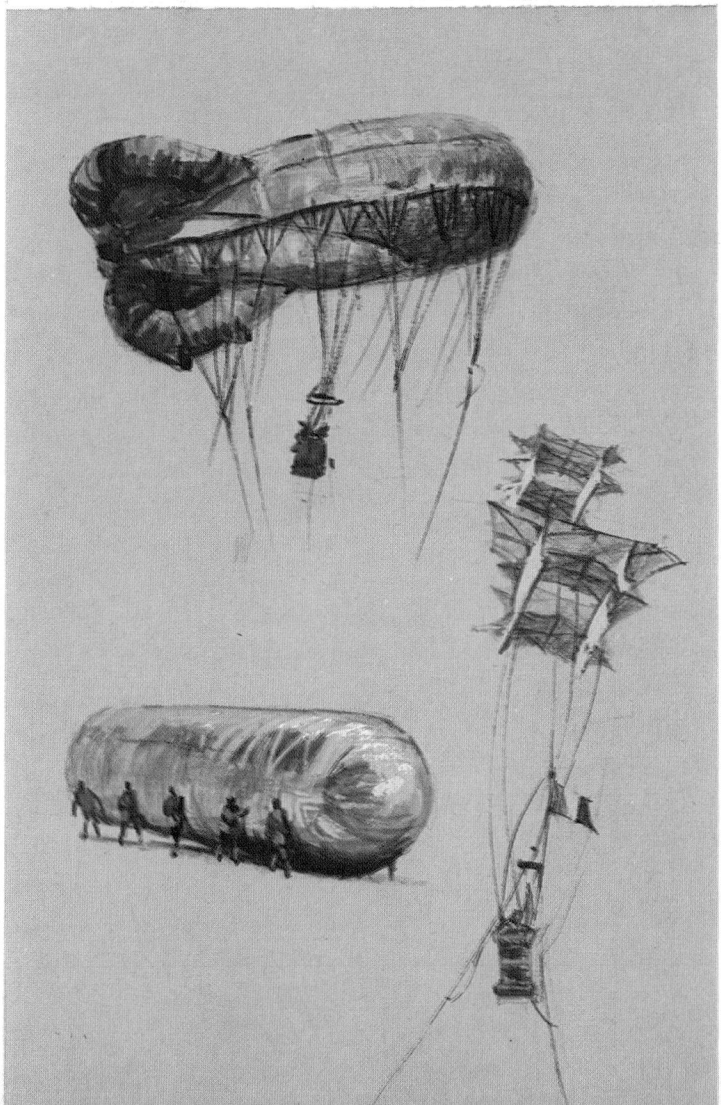

Top right: Observation balloons in the field were supplied with gas from a "nurse" balloon, tethered to the ground.

Bottom right: Box kites were also used to carry observers, but were generally not very successful.

The return of the Circus

Hauptmann Rudolf Berthold
44 victories

Leutnant Josef Veltjens
34 victories

The unit commander's primary job was to lead his men into combat and see they got back again after their patrols. The larger the formation, the more complicated this became, especially when it included a variety of aircraft.

Richthofen's Circus, the famous JGI, which travelled the length of the front with its colourful equipment, consisted of four *Jagdstaffeln*, each of 14 planes: *Jasta 2* or *Boelcke* commanded by smiling, boyish Lieutenant Wolff (30 victories), *Jasta 6* under Dostler, *Jasta 4* under Goering and *Jasta 10*, commanded briefly by Werner Voss before his tragic death. Despite their grave responsibilities, the average age of the commanders was 25, while their pilots averaged only 21!

Initially equipped with D.III Albatros fighters, the Circus was the first unit to receive the Fokker Triplane and then the D.VII. This caused complications as the speeds and fighting capacity of each model was quite different. The Triplane was slow (167kph) and highly manoeuvrable while the D.VII was fast at (188kph) and suitable for high-altitude work. The tactical solution adopted was to fly patrols at varying heights and throttle back on the faster craft so that the individual flights could come to each other's aid.

Unlike Mick Mannock, who nursed each young pilot until he felt secure as part of a team, Richthofen welcomed new pilots by telling them "The enemy will soon be here. Go up and kill some or get yourself killed!" Yet the Prussian disciplinarian never shirked his duties, particularly if he had to shepherd his flock back to their base and wait for planes in difficulty to land before he himself touched down.

The Red Baron himself once needed help. Encountering an old FE. 2B pusher one day and anticipating an

easy kill, Richthofen was surprised when a bullet from the observer's Lewis gun creased his skull, momentarily knocking him out and sending him into a spin. Recovering just in time, he wiped the blood from his eyes but had to crash-land, defended from further damage by the shocked members of his flight who had witnessed the battle. He was rushed to the hospital in Courtrai, where a few bone splinters were removed from his skull and was soon back at his favourite sport—hunting!

This was Richthofen's only wound. Guynemer was less lucky, being wounded seven times, while Nungesser was constantly in and out of hospital, returning each time and stunting madly to show that his battered body could stand the strain. Allied ace of aces René Fonck seemed to lead a charmed life, for despite his 75 victories he was *never even scratched* and only one bullet hole was ever found in any of his planes!

Medical personnel and ambulances were on constant alert at every field along the front, but wounded pilots requiring special attention suffered as much from the bumpy ride over shell-torn roads to the hospitals in the rear as they did from bullets.

In the mess

When the day's flying was over and all combat reports turned in, the pilots could finally relax. Wearily returning to their quarters, sometimes in fine French homes temporarily deserted by their owners but more often in bare Nissen huts, they changed from their flying gear into their regulation uniforms and made their way to the mess. There, clustered in small groups near the bar, they discussed the day's events, gesturing to describe some new manoeuvre they had perfected, reliving the excitement of the chase and recounting recent exploits, either their own or those of others.

After dinner, some pilots would retire to write letters home to mothers or girl friends, some played cards or chatted, and some cranked up the phonograph to play the latest hits. It became traditional in many squadrons for each pilot on leave to bring back at least one new record. Some flyers played piano or saxophone, and the commander of Albert Ball's squadron hand-picked musicians for his unit. Ball himself played violin, accompanying traditional RFC songs such as:
"The young aviator went stunting,
And as 'neath the wreckage he lay—he lay
To the mechanics assembled around him,
These last parting words did he say—he say:
(Chorus)
'Take the cylinders out of my kidneys,
The connecting rod out of my brain—my brain
From the small of my back take the crankshaft
And assemble the engine again—again!'"

Pilots never mentioned fallen comrades, but they were not forgotten. In British messes, after the customary toast to the King, the empty chairs around the table would be given their final salute.

Military Cross
(MC)

Victoria Cross
(VC)

Distinguished
Service Order
(DSO)

Farther down the line in the messes of the French *Cigognes* or *Sportifs*, the strains of *La Madelon*, *Auprès de ma blonde* or *Froufrou* rang out through the acrid smoke of black Gauloise cigarettes, punctuated by the sound of corks being popped from many a selected bottle of Burgundy or Bordeaux!

Frequently Nungesser, resplendent in full uniform and with all his medals gleaming, would summon his mechanic and driver Pochon for a brief excursion to Paris, it being understood that he would be back, if a little bleary-eyed, for the next morning's dawn patrol.

Not all had the astounding energy of the great French ace, however, and as dawn came soon most pilots were glad to get some sleep before facing the next day's battles. However, some lingered on, thinking of their lost friends. They were well aware of their chances of survival and faced the future bravely if not too optimistically, sarcastically humming the RFC 54 Squadron's famous fighting song:

"For a batman woke me from my bed;
I'd had a thick night and a very sore head
And I said to myself, to myself I said:
'Oh we haven't got a hope in the morning!'"

"Ceiling zero"

The clouds over the front line frequently fell to ground level, making flying impossible for the instrumentless planes of the time. A few pilots were kept on alert in case the weather suddenly cleared, but for the others "ceiling zero" conditions meant a chance to rest, write letters, enjoy pastimes or go and collect souvenirs. These were usually parts of the planes they had shot down. As only victories which had been confirmed by observers on the friendly side of the lines counted towards a pilot's score, a staff car or motorcycle could usually be commandeered to go in search of the wrecked planes. Many fell close to the front, so this often entailed driving for hours over shell-pocked roads and muddy fields.

Unless the enemy plane was in good enough condition to be kept intact, souvenirs included not only the crew's sidearms or clothing but also parts of the plane, especially serial numbers. Von Richthofen papered the

As Richthofen's first few victims fell behind the French lines they could not be confirmed, but he later made a practice of cutting the serial numbers from every plane he shot down.

walls of his room with these, and converted a rotary engine into an unusual chandelier. Moreover, he commemorated each victory from his first in 1916 to his 80th just before his death by having a cup inscribed with the date and the type of plane shot down.

The roundels of the Allies and the Iron Crosses of the Central Powers adorned most mess halls, though salvaged engines were usually turned over to the mechanics to be re-used. Broken propellers, many of which were of laminated oak or mahogany, could be made into unusual walking sticks, humidors, pipe racks, clockcases and even grave-markers.

Bad weather also enabled pilots to indulge in their favourite pastimes. British pilots naturally favoured cricket and tennis, and once, when the fog suddenly cleared, Albert Ball took off in his white flannels rather than change and miss the chance of a fight! A crack hunter by nature, von Richthofen kept his mess-mates well supplied with game, as did Fonck, who added local delicacies such as snails and mushrooms. Lufbery was another mushroom specialist, and cooked them to perfection, while Thaw and Bert Hall fished for trout, the former using a rod, the latter using his hands!

Every flying field had its quota of dogs and other pets. Von Richthofen sometimes took his huge Great Dane "Moritz" with him in the tiny cockpit of his triplane. *Cigogne* Captain Thénault's dog "Flam" had such a sharp sense of hearing that he could tell his master's engine and would wait for him to land.

Visitors to the *Lafayette Escadrille* were startled to find two well-grown lion cubs roaming at large. Whisky and Soda were great favourites with the pilots though they sometimes caused trouble with visiting "brass", having no respect for rank!

Strangest and perhaps the most colourful of all squadron mascots were the lion cubs kept by the *Lafayette Escadrille*. The first, "Whisky", was bought from a Brazilian dentist for 250 francs. Thaw innocently tried to bring the leashed lion back on a train, but the other travellers were so terrified that he had to be caged and carried in the goods wagon. Gentle and playful, Whisky soon grew enormous and once caused a furore by chewing up the gold-encrusted képi of a visiting French general! Whisky was soon joined by another cub, inevitably named "Soda", and Lufbery spent much of his time off romping with them. Towards the end of 1917, however, the *Escadrille's* commander decided that they were too big and too expensive to feed, and the pilots reluctantly took them to a Paris zoo. Soda did not long outlive the loss of his freedom, but even after the war Whisky would lick the hands of former *Lafayette Escadrille* pilots who came to visit him.

The bright lights

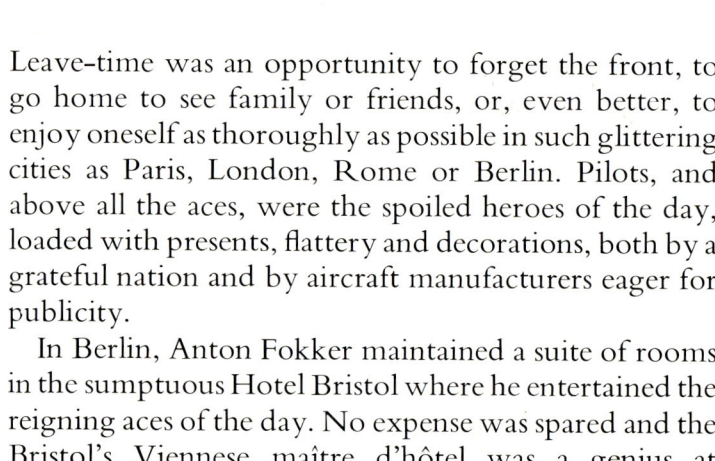

Leave-time was an opportunity to forget the front, to go home to see family or friends, or, even better, to enjoy oneself as thoroughly as possible in such glittering cities as Paris, London, Rome or Berlin. Pilots, and above all the aces, were the spoiled heroes of the day, loaded with presents, flattery and decorations, both by a grateful nation and by aircraft manufacturers eager for publicity.

In Berlin, Anton Fokker maintained a suite of rooms in the sumptuous Hotel Bristol where he entertained the reigning aces of the day. No expense was spared and the Bristol's Viennese maître d'hôtel was a genius at acquiring Dutch cheeses, Polish hams, French wines and Scotch whisky despite wartime restrictions.

After formal ceremonies to award decorations, things would become more relaxed, and though Manfred von Richthofen would pass the evening quietly sipping a single glass of wine, his brother Lothar invariably joined Goering, Sleight, Loerzer and Voss at the piano singing the latest German or Austrian refrains while Udet sketched them from a table to one side. Girls would appear, the band would strike up, and the laughter and dancing would continue far into the night until one by one the pilots would leave—some back to their homes or to romantic meetings, others back to the front.

Sometimes crowds would gather outside the Bristol, calling for their favourite aces to appear on the balcony and receive their homage. Alone, the Red Baron shunned the limelight and would retreat by a side entrance to avoid the mob. Through all these gatherings, Anton Fokker would wander with a cup of coffee, talking shop with the men who flew his planes and getting ideas for new designs.

Paris too was the scene of much merriment, and the City of Lights was thronged with every Allied uniform imaginable: the khaki of the British RFC and the US

Fokker was a genius in public relations, and made the most of his receptions at Berlin's Hotel Bristol to unveil his latest fighters.

Signal Corps (to which the Air Service belonged), field-green Italian tunics and the multi-coloured uniforms of French pilots, who wore the dress of the units to which they had belonged before becoming airmen. With their pilot's wings and many decorations (and sometimes sporting the white képi of the Foreign Legion), the pilots were easily recognized and immediately idolized, whether they were sipping an aperitif at some pavement café, going to a music-hall or boxing match or attending the opera with an elegant Parisienne.

All the aces received prize money from manufacturers for every enemy plane downed as well as invitations to sumptuous dinners. The Vanderbilts even paid a monthly allowance to supplement the pay of Americans flying with the *Lafayette Escadrille*, and Guynemer was given a magnificent sports car by Hispano-Suiza. But the gaiety and glitter had to be left behind when leave came to an end and the pilots returned to the stern task of killing or being killed.

Beside the *Légion d'Honneur* and the *Médaille Militaire,* France's leading decoration was the *Croix de Guerre.* Palms were added to this when later citations were awarded.

Légion d'Honneur   Médaille Militaire

While still a cavalryman, Nungesser captured a German staff car singlehanded, for which he received the nickname "Hussard de Mors". Punning on the make of car (Mors), he adopted a death's head (*mort* = death in French), crossed bones, coffin and candles as his personal insignia. It was painted on all his aircraft, including the *Oiseau Blanc* in which he disappeared over the Atlantic in 1927, and on the Rolls Royce in which he drove around Paris. After having to shoot down a British pilot who attacked him, mistaking his insignia for German markings, Nungesser had broad red, white and blue stripes painted on the wings of his planes.

A poet shakes an empire

When war broke out in 1914 and Italy remained neutral, poet and playwright Gabriele d'Annunzio wrote letter after letter to his homeland urging Italy to join the conflict and liberate its northern territories from Austria. But it was only after his return to Rome in May 1915 and his fiery speeches that Italy decided to fight, and the poet became a warrior. Though well over fifty, d'Annunzio immediately joined the armed forces and organized a series of propaganda raids to show the Italian colours in Austrian-held cities such as Trieste, Trento and Pola.

D'Annunzio's leaflet, in the form of an overprinted Italian flag, said (in part): "People of Vienna! We who fly over Vienna could drop bombs on you but instead drop only leaflets in three colours —the colours of liberty. . . . We Italians do not make war on children, old people or women. We make war on your government in the name of national liberty, on your cruel government which can provide you with neither peace nor bread."

His most remarkable flight, however, was to Vienna, the very heart of the Austro-Hungarian Empire, with the famous "La Sérénissima" squadron, whose planes bore the Venetian lion of St Mark. Attached directly to the Supreme Headquarters, this unit was equipped with the new SVA.5, one of the best aircraft to be produced by the Allies. A speedy single-seater with extraordinary climbing power, it had already proven its long-range capabilities with a 1,400-kilometre non-stop test flight and a 700-kilometre raid across the Alps into Germany.

On 9th August, 1918, with the poet perched uncomfortably on an auxiliary gas tank, the squadron took off and flew across the mountains to the enemy capital, circled it at an altitude of only 365 metres and dropped d'Annunzio's leaflets on its demoralized population. Then, wheeling homeward, it continued to its base and landed that same afternoon at San Pelagio after an epic flight, most of it over mountainous enemy-held territory.

Not all of d'Annunzio's raids were as innocent, however. When he was not commanding a cavalry charge, ship, submarine or infantry brigade, the poet used Gianni Caproni's remarkable trimotor to attack Austrian and German installations the length of the Adriatic.

Initially designed in 1913 in response to General Douhet's advanced theories of strategic bombing, the Caproni was a twin-boom biplane with a central cockpit, powered by three 150 h.p. Isotta-Fraschini engines, two mounted as tractors on the booms and the third as a pusher on the cockpit. With a crew of four and a maximum bomb load of 1,800 kilograms, it could stay aloft for seven hours and thus bomb distant targets. Sturdily built, its four machine guns gave it an enormous defensive power, particularly when large numbers flew in close formation. Making the most of the Caproni, in 1916 and 1917 the Italian air arm struck at the Austrian battle fleet's base at Pola, the steel mills and port facilities of Trieste, shipyards and torpedo factories in Fiume and the German submarine base at Kotor.

Strategic missions were replaced by tactical strikes after Caporetto, with Capronis bombing and strafing enemy troop concentrations behind the Piave Front and relentlessly attacking German and Austrian airfields.

One Italian bomb group also went to France at the request of the French High Command and served during the second battle of the Marne, later striking at the retreating Germans north of Reims, Thionville and Metz.

A last tribute

As the summer of 1918 turned into autumn, the Allied armies rolled inexorably forward; Austria collapsed, German forces began their retreat toward the Rhine and with them went Richthofen's Circus under the command of Hermann Goering. Ignoring Boelcke's advice, Goering took the offensive, he and his pilots flying ten hours a day in an effort to stem the tide. However, the overwhelming odds and the serious shortages of fuel, oil and ammunition took their toll. In only a few days the Circus lost 39 of its 50 available planes. At last, despite the fact that it had scored 25 victories during its last week in combat, Berlin ordered the unit back to Darmstadt where its Fokker D.VIIs were to be taken over by the Allies under the terms of the Armistice.

Mercifully, the weather over the front had deteriorated toward the end of October, grounding squadrons on both sides of the lines. As 11th November approached, Allied commanders issued orders that none of their pilots were to cross the front. At the 11th hour of the 11th day of the 11th month, returning from their last routine patrols, the pilots stunted wildly and joyfully, knowing that they would never again have to watch for an enemy diving out of the sun at them or suddenly hear the chatter of machine guns behind them.

Ground crews too celebrated that night, firing star shells and Very pistols into the sky and setting light to drums of fuel that would never again be used to power planes in combat. In every Allied capital, in London and Rome, in Brussels and Washington, people deliriously celebrated the end of the long nightmare, the conclusion of the Great War.

In Paris a giant parade down the Champs-Elysées took place on 14th July 1919. Field Marshals, Generals, bands and units from every Allied force were represented—except for the airmen! Originally, Navarre had been chosen to fly a plane beneath the Arc de Triomphe, but when he was killed in training the Prefect of Police banned all aircraft from the city and no military authority had countermanded his order. But the pilots themselves did not accept this ban, and three weeks after the parade Charles Godefroy told photographers that he would fly under the Arc the following morning.

In a Nieuport, Godefroy roared towards the massive stone arch at 160 kilometres per hour against the early

56

morning sun, quickly corrected for a sudden gust and shot through, his wings almost scraping against the stone!

Few witnessed his feat, but it was Godefroy's tribute to his colleagues—of every nationality—for whom there would be no "after-war".

Glossary

Aileron: Movable flap on the trailing edge of the wing providing control along the longitudinal axis.

Aircraft: 1. *pusher*: propeller positioned behind the cockpit (British DH.2 and FE.2B, French Farman and Voisin).
2. *tractor*: propeller in front, cockpit behind or beneath wings (French SPAD and Nieuport, British Sopwith Camel and SE5, German Albatros and Fokker).
3. *bomber*: usually with crew of two or more. Light bombers (French Bréguet 14, British DH.4, German Aviatik) were single-engined two-seaters used for tactical missions. Heavy bombers (German Gotha, Russian Sikorski, Italian Caproni, British Handley-Page) had several engines, crews of three or four men, and were used for long-range strategic bombing.
4. *fighter*: fast, manoeuvrable single-seaters (British Camel and SE.5, German Fokker Triplane, French Nieuport and SPAD).
5. *observation*: medium-sized two-seater used to direct artillery fire (French Bréguet, British Bristol Fighter).
6. *reconnaissance*: two-seaters capable of high-altitude and long-distance flying (German Rumpler, Italian SVA.9).

Artillery spotting: Directing and correcting artillery fire from an aircraft or observation balloon.

Aspect ratio: Relationship of span to chord (width) of wings.

Balloon: (Slang terms: Fr. *saucisse*; Ger. *Drachen*; Eng. gasbag, sausage). Gasbag filled with hydrogen, anchored by cables and with a place for the observer.

Biplane: Aircraft with two super-imposed wings.

Blade: One arm of a propeller.

Bomb-aimer: Crew member responsible for dropping bombs (US: *bombardier*).

Breech: Part of a machine gun into which the cartridge fits.

Bullet: 1. *incendiary*: machine gun ammunition used for setting fire to observation balloons or Zeppelins.
2. *tracer*: machine gun ammunition leaving a trail of smoke in its wake.

Carburettor: Part of an internal combustion engine in which fuel and air are mixed to form an explosive gas.

Ceiling: 1. Extreme height at which an aircraft can fly.
2. Height of clouds above the ground ("ceiling zero" = clouds at ground level).

"Cigognes": Elite French fighter group, each squadron of which had a different flying stork as its insignia.

"Circus": Elite German fighter group, particularly Richthofen's.

Climb: Rate at which an aircraft increases its altitude, measured in feet or metres per minute.

"Clock code": Radio code used in adjusting artillery fire, based on the position of clock hands: direction (3 o'clock = 90 degrees right) followed by distance (4 = 400 metres).

Confirmation: Official recognition of an air victory.

Cooling systems: 1. *air-cooled*: excess heat is lost directly into the air from fins fixed to the cylinders.
2. *liquid-cooled*: a liquid (usually water) circulates in a jacket around the cylinders and heat is lost through a radiator.

Crankcase: Metal housing protecting the moving parts of an engine.

Crankshaft: Shaft which is connected to the pistons and drives the propeller.

Dive: Descending, near-vertical flight of an aircraft.

Dope: Acetone paint used to shrink and waterproof the fabric on an aircraft; highly inflammable.

Drag: The aerodynamic force impeding the forward motion of an aircraft.

Drift: Deviation from straight flight, caused by cross-winds.

"Eindecker": German for "mono-plane", used particularly for the Fokker E.I to E.IV series of 1915-16.

Empennage (French): The tail surfaces of an aircraft (horizontal and vertical stabilizers, elevators and rudder) providing control of flight angle and direction.

Engine: 1. *in-line*: with cylinders in a row, in a V or opposed. Generally liquid-cooled.
2. *rotary*: with a fixed crankshaft, the remainder of engine and propeller rotating. Air-cooled.
3. *radial*: with cylinders radiating from a fixed crankcase. Generally air-cooled.

Fins: 1. Small metal sheets attached to the rear of a missile to give it directional stability.
2. Circular sheet metal sections projecting from the outside of a cylinder; used to increase cooling surface.

Fuselage: The body of an aircraft, to which are fixed the wings, tail, engine and landing gear, and which contains the cockpit(s).

"Grease monkey": A member of the ground crew.

Ground support: The use of aircraft to support ground troops in battle.

"Jagdgeschwader": German fighter group consisting of 4 *Jasta*; known as a JG or "Circus".

"Jasta": A German fighter squadron (short for *Jagdstaffel* = "hunting pack").

Joystick: Control lever between pilot's knees, actuating the ailerons and elevator.

Lift: Upward aerodynamic force supporting an aircraft in flight.

Longeron: Major longitudinal part of the structure of an aircraft's fuselage.

Monoplane: Aircraft with a single wing, either above the fuselage (*parasol*), central (*mid-wing*) or below it (*low-wing*).

Multi-seater: Aircraft carrying a crew of several people (usually a heavy bomber).

Propeller: Drive unit in the form of and acting as an air screw, pushing or pulling the aircraft (*pusher* or *tractor*). Usually two- or four-bladed.

Rib: Longitudinal member attached to the wing spars and forming the aerodynamic shape (*camber*) which creates lift.

Rigging: The system of wires and struts used to give rigidity to an aircraft's structure.

Rudder: Vertical flap at rear of aircraft actuated by the rudder bar and providing directional control.

Rudder bar: Pivoted horizontal bar enabling the pilot to steer with his feet.

Sesquiplane: Aircraft with normal upper wing and small lower wing, combining the advantages of a monoplane and biplane.

Single-seater: Aircraft with room only for a pilot; usually a fighter.

Span: The distance between wing tips.

Spin: Manoeuvre in which the plane has lost flying speed (*stalled*) and spins downwards out of control.

Squadron: Combat unit, usually comprising 14 fighters (Ger. *Jagdstaffel*; Fr. *escadrille*; It. *squadriglia*).

Struts: Metal or wooden bars used to join the lifting surfaces (wings); arranged in a star, N or V.

Synchronization: Mechanical and/or hydraulic system enabling bullets from a machine gun to pass between the propeller blades.

Torque: Gyroscope force generated by spinning rotary engine or propeller, which makes an aircraft turn on its longitudinal axis.

Triplane: Aircraft with three superimposed wings.

Truss: Triangulated system of struts and wires giving rigidity to a structure.

Two-seater: Aircraft with room for two (pilot and observer-gunner).

Wing surfaces: Area of wings providing lift.

Wing-warping: Twisting the wings, with cables, to give control along the plane's longitudinal axis. Replaced by *ailerons*.

Wires: 1. *landing*: wires supporting the wings when aircraft is on the ground.
2. *control*: wires connecting joystick and rudder bar to control surfaces.
3. *flying*: wires absorbing lift forces while aircraft is in flight.

Zeppelin: Large German-built rigid airship used mainly for mass bombing raids.

Main events

1914

June 28 Austro-Hungarian Crown Prince assassinated at Sarajevo.

July 28 Austria-Hungary declares war on Serbia.

Aug. 1 Germany declares war on Russia.

Aug. 3 Germany declares war on France.

Aug. 4 Britain declares war on Germany. Immelmann flies over Paris in a Taube.

Aug. 6 Austria-Hungary declares war on Russia.

Aug. 13-15 RFC squadrons to France.

Aug. 22 German advance on Mons noted by RFC patrols.

Aug. 25 First plane (German) forced to land (by 3 RFC planes).

Sept. 4-6 French patrols report eastward movement of German army.

Sept. 6-10 First battle of the Marne.

Sept. 22 British bomb Zeppelin hangars.

Oct. 5 First aerial victory: Franz and Quénault shoot down an Aviatik.

Oct. 21 Samson bombs the Zeppelin factory at Friedrichshafen.

Oct. 29 Turkey declares war on Allies.

Oct. 30 First Battle of Ypres.

Dec. 16 First aerial attack on Britain.

1915

Jan. First aerial photo-reconnaissance and artillery spotting missions.

Jan. 19-20 First Zeppelin attack on Britain.

Feb. 5 RFC 11, first all-fighter squadron formed. Garros downs 5 German planes, shooting through his propeller.

April 17 First Belgian air victory: Jacquet shoots down an Aviatik.

April 19 Garros captured, with his plane.

April 22 Second battle of Ypres; first use of poison gas (by Germans).

May 7 *Lusitania* sunk by German U-boat. Fokker presents synchronization.

May 23 Italy declares war on Austria.

May 26 Oswald Boelcke's first victory.

May 31 First Zeppelin raid on London.

June 7 First Zeppelin shot down.

July 19 Guynemer's first victory.

July 25 Lanoe Hawker in a Bristol Scout shoots down 3 enemy aircraft.

Aug. 12 First ship sunk by aircraft.

Aug. 20 Italy declares war on Turkey.

Oct. 14 Bulgaria declares war on Allies.

Nov. 3 First military take-off from an aircraft carrier (the *Vindex*).

Dec. 25 Richthofen receives pilot's wings. Guynemer awarded *Légion d'Honneur*.

1916

Jan. First air patrols in formation.

Jan. 29-31 Zeppelin raids on Paris.

Feb. 21 Battle of Verdun begins.

March Ernst Udet's first victory.

March 9-15 Portugal joins Allies.

March 21 Squadron of American volunteers formed (core of *Lafayette Escadrille*).

April Zeppelin shot down by rocket.

April 7 Baracca's first victory.

April 14 RNAS planes bomb Constantinople.

April 20 Elliott Cowdin becomes the first American pilot to be awarded France's *Médaille Militaire*.

May 16 Nungesser, in a Voisin, shoots down an Aviatik over Nancy, is awarded *Croix de Guerre* and given eight days' detention for insubordination!

May 24 Lufbery joins volunteer American squadron.

May 31 Battle of Jutland.

July First tracer bullets used.

July 1 Battle of the Somme begins.

July 30 First joint operations of French and British air forces.

Aug. Boelcke forms the first *Jagdstaffel*.

Aug. 27 Rumania and Italy join Allies.

Sept. 6 McCudden's first victory.

Sept. 13-26 Capronis bomb Trieste.

Sept. 23 Guynemer shoots down 3 aircraft.

Oct. 28 Boelcke killed.

Nov. 23 Richthofen shoots down Hawker.

Nov. 28 Gothas bomb London.

Dec. 12 RFC authorized strength raised to 106 regular, 95 reserve squadrons.

1917

March 17 René Fonck's first victory.

March 25 Billy Bishop's first victory.

April 2 Richthofen's first double.

April 6 USA declares war on Germany.

May 6 Ball's 44th and last victory. Mannock's first victory, a balloon.

May 15 Pétain made French C-in-C.

May 20 First submarine sunk by a plane.

May 24 France asks USA for 5,000 pilots, 50,000 mechanics and 4,500 planes.

May 25 Guynemer shoots down 4 planes.

June 2 Billy Bishop achieves a triple.

June 26 First *Jagdgeschwader* formed.

July 4 First "Liberty" engine made.

Aug. 2 First landing of an aircraft (Sopwith Pup) on a warship.

Aug. 14 China joins Allies.

Aug. 31 Third battle of Ypres begins.

Sept. 11 Guynemer lost over Poelcapelle.

Sept. 17 Lothar von Richthofen's first victory.

Oct. 14 RFC forms 41st Bomb Wing for the strategic bombing of German industry.

Oct. 21 Baracca's first double.

Oct. 24 Battle of Caporetto.

Nov. 15 Scaroni's first victory.

Nov. 20 Battle of Cambrai.

Dec. 15 Armistice between USSR and Germany.

Dec. 26 Scaroni's first triple.

1918

Feb. 6 McCudden shoots down 4 aircraft.

March 21-24 German offensive on Western Front.

March 29 Foch made Allied C-in-C.

April 1 RFC and RNAS combined to form RAF. First American air victories, by Winslow and Campbell.

April 16 Willy Coppens de Houthulst downs his first balloon.

April 21 Death of Manfred von Richthofen.

April 29 Rickenbacker's first victory.

May 9 Lufbery dies. Nungesser scores a double. Fonck's first sextuple.

May 20-31 Rickenbacker and Campbell become the first American aces.

June 6 Bombing of Germany by the British Independent Air Force begins.

June 19 Baracca downed by ground fire.

July 5 Hermann Goering assumes command of Richthofen's Circus.

July 26 Mannock shot down and killed.

Aug. 2-8 Last Zeppelin raid on England. Second Battle of the Somme.

Sept. 10-27 Frank Luke downs 21 balloons. American offensive near Saint Mihiel supported by 1,451 aircraft.

Sept. 25 Rickenbacker attacks 7 German aircraft and is put in command of 94th Aero Squadron.

Sept. 26 Fonck scores another sextuple.

Oct. 14 British Handley-Page bomber drops 800-kilogram bomb, heaviest of the war.

Oct. 27 William Barker, alone in a Snipe, fights off 60 enemy planes.

Oct. 31 Turkey surrenders.

Nov. 1-10 Austria surrenders to Italy.

Nov. 11 Armistice signed at 11 a.m.

Index

WESTERN FRONT 1915-1918

AIRFIELDS
 German-Austrian
American
British
Belgian
French
Italian

ENGLAND

London

Canterbury
Dover
Folkestone
Dunkirk
Southampton
Calais
St Pol
Brighton
Boulogne

Auxi Le Château
Abbeville

ITALIAN FRONT 1915-1918

Friedrichshafen
(Zeppelin factory)

Innsbruck

AUSTRIA

Vaduz

Lienz

SWITZERLAND

Coire

Merano

ISONZO FRONT
(pre-October 1917)

Bolzano

Caporetto
(retreat)

St Moritz

Belluno

Udine

Feltre

Trent

Gorizja

Bassano

Como

PIAVE FRONT
(post-October 1917)

Istrana

Fiume

Trieste

Bergamo

Vicenza

Venice

Verona

Padua

Pola

Milan

ITALY

Marconi

Givesnes

Estrées S

Beauvais

Le Pl